The Day They Padlocked the Church

Pastor Sileven and 1,000 Christians Who Defied Nebraska Tyranny in America's Crisis of Freedom: An Eyewitness Account

H. Edward Rowe

HUNTINGTON HOUSE, INC.
1200 N. MARKET STREET, SUITE G
SHREVEPORT, LOUISIANA 71107
(318) 222-1350

Third Printing 1983

Copyright © 1983 by Huntington House, Inc.
Printed in the United States of America
ISBN 0-910311-05-6

Dedication

To Everett and Tressie Sileven, the members of Faith Baptist Church, and the students of Faith Christian School.

May their valiant biblical stand arouse millions to action against the rising tide of state tyranny in America.

Introduction
by D. James Kennedy, Ph.D.

The cataclysmic events which Edward Rowe reports in this book should deeply concern every American.

Nebraska's persecution of Pastor Everett Sileven and other Christians makes a tragic mockery of a nation conceived explicitly to banish such medieval brutality.

The great First Amendment to our United States Constitution clearly restrains government from prohibiting the free exercise of religion. The refusal of Nebraska's legislature and judiciary to be guided by this principle betrays nothing less than a staggering failure of leadership.

Christian parents are under an undisputed biblical mandate to rear and educate their children. The Bible makes it clear that children belong to their parents as a sacred stewardship responsibility, and not to the state.

Tyrants have always desired to possess the children and to mold their young minds in the image of the anti-God state. "Your child belongs to us," declared Adolph Hitler in 1933.

Beginning with gradual subtlety, the Hitler-controlled state took over the children. "The new Reich will give to its youth its own education and its own upbringing," said Hitler in 1937.

Shortly after that, criminal prosecution of parents began. If parents refused to surrender their children to the Hitler youth movement to be indoctrinated in Nazism, they were taken forcibly from their parents and given to the state.

In 1936 Hitler abolished all Christian schools in Germany. In 1938 all teachers were ordered to resign from any religious organization. Control of education had run its course. The youth of Germany — body, soul and spirit — had been seized by the secular state.

The claim of Nebraska officials that they really intend no control of church-operated Christian schools is empty on the face of it. If no control is intended, why require state approval of such schools and state certification of their teachers?

The power to approve is at once the power to disapprove. The power to certify is the power not to certify. Such powers amount to the power of the state to control religious school ministry and, therefore, religion itself. No amount of legal jargon, no judicial trickery, can ever change this fact.

Acting in the wake of the Nazi tyranny of five decades ago, the secular establishment of Nebraska now moves gradually to seize control of church-operated religious education.

Ed Rowe's moving account of the events of September and October 1982 must be read by every American who values his freedom.

No reader of this book will emerge uninstructed concerning the critical issue of religious liberty, or uninspired to act resolutely on behalf of it.

— January 1983

Author's Preface

Thousands of pages would be required to chronicle the struggle which has raged for half a dozen years between the marshalled political, legal and police powers of Nebraska and Pastor Everett Sileven of Louisville.

Nebraska's case against Sileven and Faith Baptist Church is stated in an action filed by Nebraska Attorney General Paul L. Douglas on April 24, 1979.

Douglas and Cass County Attorney Ronald D. Moravec charged Pastor Sileven, Mrs. Sileven, Faith Christian School, and seven teachers and officials of the school with the following nine specific violations of Nebraska School Laws:

1. Failure to submit reports to the state.

2. Failure of the school administrators to submit to state administrative certification.

3. Failure of teachers to submit to state teaching certification.

4. Failure to register state administrative or teaching certificates in the county office.

5. Failure to render a Fall Approval Report to the State Department of Education.

6. Failure to submit to the State Department of Education the college credits earned by each teacher at Faith Christian School.

7. Failure to seek "initial approval status" from the state, as an "approved school system."

8. Failure to comply with rules and regulations of the State Department of Education.

9. Failure to comply with Nebraska laws for operation of a private school.

All of these charges are based on enacted state regulations which are both unbiblical and unconstitutional, as this book will demonstrate.

A relentless war is being waged by all of the legal and armed might of Nebraska against a pastor, a small church and its tiny school in Louisville, a town of less than one thousand people all but lost among the expansive cornfields of Eastern Nebraska.

This particular battle took place in September and October of 1982. I report the major episodes of the struggle during this particular period as lucidly and accurately as possible. I do so to warn Americans of the rising threat to religious liberty in this country.

I wrote this book toward the end of 1982 during my term of service as Executive Director of Coral Ridge Ministries — Dr. D. James Kennedy's television organization in Fort Lauderdale. Shortly after completing the script, I accepted a call to become President and Chief Administrative Officer of the Church League of America which is headquartered in Wheaton, Illinois.

America today is flirting with tyranny. The pattern in Nebraska is strikingly similar to certain developments in Germany during the fourth decade of this century.

Our only hope as a nation lies in a mass movement of godly pastors and biblically committed citizens.

May God use this book to awaken His people to the impending peril — and to the staggering responsibility which they must assume — if America is to gain victory over the spirit of statism and tyranny which this nation was founded to vanquish forever.

— H. Edward Rowe
Wheaton, Illinois
January 1983

Acknowledgements

Sincere thanks to my wife, Lois, and to my administrative assistant, Linda Alexander, for typing the manuscript of this book.

— Edward Rowe
January 1983

Contents

1. Pastor Sileven and State Tyranny 1
2. A Hundred Who Stood 8
3. Swamped in a Storm 24
4. Point of No Retreat 29
5. Justice and the Judge 36
6. Victory Will Come 55
7. The Pen and Ink Debate 59
8. Occupy for Christ 79

About the Author 83

1
Pastor Sileven
and State Tyranny

"We ought to obey God rather than men" (Acts 5:29).

Louisville is a tranquil town of about a thousand people nestled among the cornfields of beautiful Eastern Nebraska. There the sounds of the songbirds and insects of summer blend with the bustle of happy people working their farms — and others going about the tasks of the town.

A dozen miles down the road is Plattsmouth, a town of some nine thousand people. It is the administrative and judicial seat of Cass County, and it is the base from which an act of state tyranny was perpetrated against a man of God in sleepy Louisville. It happened on "Black Friday," September 3, 1982.

On that day Cass County Sheriff Fred Tesch and Deputy Larry Shelborn, acting on a bench warrant issued on September 2 by Judge Raymond J. Case, drove out to Louisville from Plattsmouth and arrested a man of God while ministering in the pulpit of his church and locked him in a jail tank with common criminals. The man of

1

God is Dr. Everett Sileven, Pastor of Faith Baptist Church of Louisville.

The reason for the arrest and jailing of Sileven? He and the members of Faith Baptist Church had chosen to "obey God rather than men" (Acts 5:29) and to open and operate a school for the education of their children in obedience to the Word of God. The problem was that this contravened a court order to close down the educational aspect of the church's ministry.

The state of Nebraska had enacted legislation requiring all schools, including those operated as an integral function of the ministry of a church, to submit to state certification and approval of administrators and teachers, and to comply with "rules and regulations of the State Department of Education."

Inasmuch as it is an axiom of history that the power to approve is the power to control, and the power to control is the power to destroy, Pastor Sileven and the members of Faith Baptist Church decided to continue educating their children in obedience to God, without the approval of the secular establishment of Nebraska.

Sileven and the people of Faith Baptist Church believe they are bound by Deuteronomy 6:6-9 and other biblical passages to assume full responsibility under God for the education of their children, as a direct and inseparable function of their church. They believe the state of Nebraska confronted them with a clear choice: In order to obey Nebraska, they would need to disobey God. This they would not do.

Further, they believe they are protected by the First Amendment to the United States Constitution from governmental regulation of their religious faith and practice, and from any governmental limitation of its "free exercise."

The jailing of a pastor for serving his God in accordance with the dictates of his biblically directed conscience is an act of tyranny which is unthinkable in our supposedly free constitutional republic.

Webster's New World Dictionary defines *tyranny* as "oppressive and unjust government, cruel and unjust use of power or authority."

The long arm of state tyranny has brazenly interfered with the spiritual ministry of a church that is explicitly dedicated to the service of God and the betterment of man.

The local community and the nation have been deprived of the rich benefits of the wholesome and constructive services of a minister of Christ.

State tyranny has deprived a good woman of her husband, a good man of his wife, a family of its head, a church of its pastor, and children of spiritual leadership.

State tyranny has imposed upon a good and godly man a fate which should be reserved for robbers, rogues and criminals.

State tyranny has dishonored an honorable man.

State tyranny has invaded the church, a sanctuary of the Sovereign God of the universe. Uniformed and armed police offended innocent little children, frightening them into tearful sobbing as their spiritual leader was arrested and taken away right before their eyes!

State tyranny has blatantly violated the supreme law of our land, prohibited the free exercise of religion, and trampled on the Bible, the flag and the Constitution.

State tyranny has re-enacted the horrors of Nazi Germany in the fourth decade of this century, when uniformed men seized godly pastors in their churches, hauled them away and locked them up.

Like the executioners who nailed our Lord Jesus Christ to the cross, the armed officers of a corrupt and degraded establishment acted on orders from a "higher authority," trampling in contempt the very founding principles of America.

The Nazi war criminals, who perpetrated the most awful atrocities against harmless and helpless people, responded to charges with the statement, "I acted under orders from my superiors; therefore I am not to blame for what I did."

The Nuremberg judges, who were regarded as the preeminent legal minds of that era in the field of criminal law, refused to accept the "orders from the boss" cop-out as a justifiable excuse for the perpetration of monstrous evils against harmless persons. The lives of those who perpetrated those evil acts were squeezed out by the hangman's noose, pursuant to the processes of justice.

While no reasonable person would allege that the arrest and jailing of Pastor Everett Sileven on September 3, 1982, was in the same league with the deeds of the war criminals, multitudes will maintain that it was the same *in principle*.

Those who perpetrated that act sinned shamefully against God. They contributed to the alarming trend to deny Americans their constitutional freedoms, and to bring down on the heads of helpless and harmless citizens the overspreading horrors of the police state.

In jailing Pastor Sileven for his refusal to disobey his God, Nebraska relied upon the arrogant brute power of the state as a means of dealing with biblically based Christian conscience.

Nebraska sought by force of the police state to accomplish what the lions of the Coliseum, the cross of execution, the sword, the axe, the guillotine, the burning stake and the torture chamber were powerless to accomplish long centuries ago.

Imprisonment offers no inducement to violate the will of God. Death holds no terror to those who would rather die than live in bondage under state tyranny.

Every genuine Christian is duty-bound to "obey God rather than men" (Acts 5:29) whenever the ordinances of men are in conflict with the clearly expressed will of God.

The immortal First Amendment, which forbids laws regulating religion and prohibiting its "free exercise," was written into our Constitution to preclude any such conflict. Those who voted to adopt this provision had heard the unanimous voice of history that the sword and the gun, wielded by the tyrant state, cannot possibly subdue and dominate biblically based Christian conscience.

How many men and women of God is Nebraska prepared to commit to the dungeon in its determination to shackle Christian conscience pertaining to the rearing and education of children?

Will Nebraska persist until it has been reduced to a Nazi-style police state?

Will the power elite of Nebraska sleep well to the clanging of iron jailhouse gates and the crying of wives and little children?

Sheriff Fred Tesch of Cass County cannot escape personal responsibility for the arrest and jailing of Pastor Sileven. County Prosecutor Ronald Moravec cannot escape responsibility for that evil deed. Judge Raymond J. Case, who issued the order for the arrest, cannot escape responsibility. Attorney General Paul Douglas cannot escape responsibility.

The Nebraska State Department of Education cannot escape responsibility. The Nebraska Legislature cannot escape responsibility. The citizens of Nebraska who elected the legislators cannot escape responsibility for this horrendous violation of the most elementary rules of decency and civility.

Writing in the distinguished *Nebraska Law Review* (Vol. 61, No. 1), Timothy J. Binder has rebuked Nebraska for the heavy-handed treatment which Sileven and Faith Baptist Church have received at the hands of that state.

According to Binder, such treatment of harmless people who are conscience-bound to obey God represents "a severe blow to religious freedom in Nebraska." Further, writes Binder, it is "contrary to the free exercise test which has evolved through United States Supreme Court decisions."

Author Binder proceeded to sound an enlightened warning, which should be heard and heeded by every tyrant from coast to coast: The action of Nebraska, writes Binder, "will unnecessarily place individuals in a position where they must make a choice between their God and their government; it will not be unreasonable for those individuals to choose to obey their God and suffer punishment at the hands of the government."

The Plattsmouth tyranny will live long in the annals of shame and infamy. It has warned Americans everywhere of the overspeeding dangers of the encroaching tyranny of the state.

Awake, pastors! Awake, Christians! Awake, Americans! Arise in the power of the Word of God and the Holy Spirit! Sound the alarm! Spread the word! Shout from every village, city and farm the warning of impending state tyranny!

Finally, my brethren, be strong in the Lord and in the power of his might.

Put on the whole armor of God, that you may be able to stand against the wiles of the devil.

For we do not wrestle against flesh and blood, but against principalities, against powers, against the rulers of the darkness of this age, against spiritual wickedness in the heavenly places.

Therefore take up the whole armor of God, that you may be able to withstand in the evil day, and having done all, to stand (Ephesians 6:10-13).

2

A Hundred Who Stood

"Stand fast therefore in the liberty wherewith Christ hath made us free . . ." (Galatians 5:1).

It is a long night in Louisville, Nebraska. A hundred pastors from fourteen states maintain a watchful vigil inside Faith Baptist Church. A court order has been signed by District Judge Raymond J. Case, demanding the chaining and padlocking of the church in order to close its tiny Christian day school.

The mood of the pastors is sober. Legal options have been exhausted. The church's pastor, Dr. Everett Sileven, has been incarcerated in Cass County Jail, Plattsmouth, since September 3. His offense: operating the school without the approval of the Nebraska Department of Education. Now the purpose of this all-night meeting of pastors on October 17-18 is to take a firm stand for the biblical and constitutional principle of non-interference by the state in the religious ministry of the church.

A hundred men of God have stepped aside from their routine duties and gathered on very short notice.

Judge Case has offered to unlock the church if its leaders will only move the school into a neighboring county. The church board has declined on principle. A frontal collision between state tyranny and biblically based Christian conviction is clearly inevitable.

In a Sunday evening strategy meeting it is decided unanimously that we will occupy the church in the face of a court order to chain and padlock its doors. The order provides that the church will be locked by Cass County Sheriff Fred Tesch and his deputies any time after midnight on the morning of October 18, 1982.

We resolve that we will not vacate the house of God. We will be on our knees in prayer when the police arrive. We will respond to no orders to vacate. This is God's territory. Why should we abandon it to state forces which are acting unconstitutionally?

After five and a half years of unsuccessful legal combat we will draw the line. We will retreat not an inch, no matter what the consequences.

The clock ticks off the early hours of October 18. When will they come? What will they do? There is a rumor that the police will arrive "around 2:00 p.m." No show. Only an occasional sheriff's car cruises past the church. We keep singing and preaching. Some of us recline on the cold floor in a vain attempt to steal a wink of sleep. The clock just ticks and ticks and ticks. The dark shadow of inevitability looms.

Thirty-nine-year-old Pastor Richard Moore of Idaho, former police officer for eight years, tells the waiting pastors what can happen.

"Refusal to vacate is cause for arrest," he warns. "If an officer touches your body, he must arrest you. They can hit you with heavy charges. If they throw the book at you, it can mean a year in jail."

Still we resolve to ignore any order to vacate. If we're going out, they'll have to throw us out. It means certain arrest.

Richard Moore is as firm as any.

But "It's scary," he confesses.

It is 2:59 a.m. The phone rings. Assistant Pastor Phil Schmidt answers. It's Sheriff Tesch.

"Captain Syslo of the State Patrol and I are here at the Louisville Police Station. If you want to talk about the situation, we're inviting you to bring a couple of the leaders over," the sheriff says.

Pastor Schmidt quickly asks Dr. Greg Dixon, Pastor of the Indianapolis Baptist Temple, and me to come along.

I suggest we invite Pastor Rich Moore to join us, because of his police background and consequent understanding of the "other side." We rush to Phil's car and take off for the one-mile drive.

We park in the early morning darkness, half a block upstreet from the fire station. The glare of a battery of TV camera lights is exaggerated by the foreboding cloud cover.

Entering the Fire Station, the two law officers introduce themselves by name, and so do we.

At 3:08 a.m. we sit down around a shabby conference table.

Flanked by Greg on my right and Phil on my left, I am straight across the table from Sheriff Tesch. To the left of Phil, at table-end, sits Captain R. Syslo, head of a fourteen-county section of the Nebraska State Patrol. Ex-policeman Rich Moore, probably due to his officer instinct, sits with his back to the wall between Syslo and Tesch.

The sheriff of Cass County opens the discussion.

"We invited you down here because you are leaders of your group, and we thought we might avoid some trouble by talking. We have a court order to lock the church, and we're going to have to do it. Will you ask your men to vacate the premises so that we can proceed?" he asks.

We speedily assure the officers that we will do no such thing.

"That church is a sovereign embassy of Jesus Christ," says Greg. "You have no right to interfere with its religious ministry."

TV cameras shoot the scene through the glass door of the room as Tesch launches into a mild rage.

"You're breaking the law! You've come here from all over the country to break the law of Nebraska! Sileven is a lawbreaker, and so are you! You guys are just out for publicity! I'm getting tired of all this!" he yells.

His outburst increases in volume as it continues.

"I know who you are, Rowe, I have that letter you wrote to me after we put Sileven in jail. It's on file in my office. I remember those fifteen reasons you gave to show how wrong I was to put Sileven in jail on September 3," he blurts.

"I don't retract one syllable of that letter!" I interject.

"I had a court order to jail Sileven," Tesch resumes. "I've taken an oath to carry out the orders of the court! And that's exactly what I'm going to do again!"

He grabs up the court order from the table and shakes it.

I sit in amazement as this armed man of the law discharges himself of this verbal barrage, blurting out bitterness over his bulging flak jacket. My eyes fall to the ponderous wooden handle of his revolver. It occurs to me that it's less than totally safe for a man who can't control his temper to have a loaded deadly weapon two inches from his elbow.

It's Greg Dixon's turn. With his Bible open, he aims a witness at the bullyish-looking sheriff, warning of the judgment of God upon all who do not repent.

"Oh now, don't try to scare me with that stuff," interrupts the Sheriff of Cass. "I don't go for that at all. I am a religious man myself. My grandchild goes to a parochial school. And it's a *certified* one, too!"

Greg tries to expound the thirteenth chapter of Romans to show the sheriff how tragically he violates his duty when he suppresses *good* works rather than *evil*. I scrutinize the visage of the man across the table. Anxiety, nervousness, defensiveness, arrogance, bitterness — all of these liabilities burden his countenance. A sense of pity grips my heart.

Again and again Tesch interrupts Greg, whose scriptural darts, masterfully interjected, strike on target. Greg might as well talk to the north wind, I conclude. The sheriff isn't hearing a thing.

To my left at the end of the table, Captain Syslo has waited in silence. Softly and with warmth, he takes the floor.

"Gentlemen, I'd like to tell you why I'm here. From time to time the Sheriff's Department in one of our counties has some requirement for additional personnel in order to fulfill a responsibility. Sheriff Tesch has asked me to come in, just in case there's a need for some extra assistance," he says.

Instantly I am drawn to the reasonable demeanor of the fiftyish man with the grey mustache. I like him. I want desperately to comply with his wishes. But I know I cannot.

"This very day is the thirty-third anniversary of my

career in law enforcement," he continues, "and I assure you I've never experienced anything like this!"

"And we know why," retorts Greg. "It demonstrates how far this country has moved in the direction of state domination of religion!"

The captain listens understandingly.

"The First Amendment to our U.S. Constitution says you can't do what you're about to do," I interject. "We have no choice but to take our stand on constitutional ground. It's only because people just like us have resisted tyranny at certain crossroads of history, that any of us at this table have any freedom at all today."

Captain Syslo now asks a thoughtful question which relates back to Greg's reference to the church as a "sovereign embassy of Jesus Christ."

"Do you men believe the church is a sanctuary against any crime?" he asks.

Instantly I reply, "By no means! The basic functions of government are the protection of life, liberty and property. If a church property is used for the making of Molotov cocktails to be thrown into police cars or homes, the police forces of the government must move in and put a stop to it. When they do, we pastors will certainly side with the police!

"But this present case at Faith Baptist Church is different. Here the state seeks to interfere with a very basic tenet of our religious faith. No crime is involved. It is for acts of righteousness in the performance of our religious faith that the court has ordered the chaining and padlocking of the church. We have no alternative but to resist, and we believe the correctness of our cause will be established in due course."

Captain Syslo listens quietly, attentively. He is a

thoughtful man. Now he speaks:

"You men have deeply held Christian convictions. But do you realize what charges can be pressed against you?"

"Disobeying the lawful order of a police officer, contempt of court, and failure to comply," says Rich Moore. "You can hit us hard."

"Do all of your men realize that?" asks the captain.

"Yes, they do," Rich replies. "I told them all about it in a briefing. They are taking a stand in the face of the clear threat of arrest and jailing. But let me ask you, Captain, are you prepared to put a hundred men in jail? Maybe three or four hundred before this is over?"

"We just don't have the room to put up that many people," admitted the captain without hesitation.

Assistant Pastor Phil Schmidt speaks up, expressing bewilderment about the whole situation and defending Pastor Sileven.

Sheriff Tesch launches into yet another tirade, this time castigating Sileven.

"He staged that chapel meeting when I arrested him on September 3!" he shouted. "He did it all for the cameras and publicity!"

"You had the guns; we had no weapons," Greg explains. "We wanted the world to see just what you are. Your actions were exposed to the light of day. You arrested a man of God in his pulpit, right in the act of performing his spiritual duties. We exacted the highest possible price from you. We let you show the world just what you are."

By now Sheriff Tesch is fuming with anger and frustration. Every time he opens his mouth, he runs into a withering blast of verbal truth and logic. I watch his reactions.

He's accustomed to being at the top of the heap, I observe to myself. Because he can't rule the scene, he's beside himself. So I decide to plunge the verbal dagger a final time.

"May I ask you a technical question, Sheriff? One of our researchers has turned up some behind-the-scenes information that raises a serious question about your personal role in coming out here to Louisville to lock up this church. I'm reliably informed that you need not do it if you don't want to. Is this correct?" I ask.

I look the sheriff straight in the eyes. He is furious. He's been found out. Now he knows that we will hold him personally responsible for what he is about to do. Until now, he's been hiding behind the court order which he frequently picks up and shakes. He can no longer hide. We have his number. He pauses and peers back, obviously rounding up words for his reply.

"Well, *this* sheriff *will* enforce *this* court order!" he blurts, with eyes flashing.

That's it. The sheriff now wants us out of there so that he can do his deed. He stands up. Beaten in every verbal skirmish, frustrated to the core of his being, and short of temper, he blurts his conclusion.

"There's no point in talking any more," he fumes.

We know what he means, and we leave.

Lurking outside the door, the television camera crews ask what happened in the meeting.

I stop momentarily and reply, "Nothing happened except for discussion. We yielded not an inch. Neither did they. It's a stalemate. We're going back now to resume our positions in the church."

With that, the four of us break into a run for our waiting car. Phil does a fast loop in the abandoned street and we shoot back to Faith Baptist Church.

Greg suggests that I report to the group on the meeting.
I stand at the pulpit. It is just past 4:30 a.m. Apologizing that my head isn't working just right due to sleeplessness and fatigue, I proceed to share with the assembled pastors the highlights of the confrontation just concluded.

The group is fully supportive. Not a man flinches. Not an objection is raised. I look into the eyes of those who are certainly among the cream of American manhood. I cannot imagine these good and honorable men subjected to humiliation. But something has to give.

Again the clock ticks. We await the inevitable. We are certain that we will be arrested, for they cannot clear us out of the church without handling our bodies. And if they do that, they *must* place us under arrest. Otherwise they violate our civil rights, says Rich Moore.

Some of us again try to get some sleep on the floor. I lie beside the pastor's desk in his study, my suitcoat over my chest as a very inadequate blanket. The phone keeps ringing. There is commotion. People talking. No way to sleep. We have no idea when to expect zero hour.

I return to the auditorium. There is singing and fellowship. I stand and address the group.

"If you think *you* have a problem, just think what a problem *they* have!" I say.

I call Lois.

"I can't believe what's happening."

I pause to control myself as the unthinkable plight of America seizes me. Emotion boils up close to the surface from deep within. I am shocked beyond belief that this is taking place in America.

There is singing in the auditorium. How long will it

continue? The men have agreed to hit the floor on their knees and to pray aloud, each individually, as soon as our watchmen report the arrival of the sheriff and his men.

Suddenly, from the pastor's study where I'm talking to my wife long distance, I discern a change of sound in the auditorium. The singing has stopped. The men are praying!

"Got to go!" I tell Lois.

I slam the phone down, dash out the study door, through the hallway to the right and into the auditorium. No uniformed officers in sight.

Quickly I take my place, kneeling over the second pew from the front. To my left is Rich Moore, praying aloud as are all the other men, individually.

I add my voice to the prayers of the others. I resolve not to open my eyes or look around. Further, I determine within myself that if I'm to go out of that church, every last ounce of my body will have to be *carried* out. I will not aid the process of vacating the church.

If they jail me I will not accept their bond, eat their food or drink their water. I know what horrors tyranny can inflict. It nailed my Lord Jesus Christ to the cross. I will not cooperate with tyranny. I would rather die than live under its soul-crushing dominion.

These moments are purifying to my life as I contemplate the corridor of torture into which the Savior entered voluntarily. No turning back. He did it for me. New insights rush into my head.

"This is just a tiny bit of what He faced," I repeat to myself.

I thank Him for setting His course straight into the darkness that is death and hell — for absorbing not only the shame and the pain, but especially for bearing in His own sinless person the just penalty for my sins and for the sins of the entire race of fallen humanity.

"He did it for me," I remind myself. "How can I not give my whole being to Him in this small crisis — at this crossroads skirmish in the struggle for freedom?

"Lord, I thank You for the privilege of taking this stand for You."

Some fifteen to twenty minutes pass. Suddenly — a heavy-handed tug on my left shoulder. Someone gets under my armpits.

"Get his legs," a deputy says.

My body is lifted horizontally, and I feel myself being carried. Presently I'm lying full-length on the ground — in the dark.

I open my eyes and look straight up into the face of 39-year-old Pastor Rich Moore. He's brushing himself off. He peers down at me sprawled on the ground in my best suit. The scene strikes him funny.

"Come on, Rowe, let's not be so dramatic about it," he says.

We laugh. I get up on my feet and look around.

We've been dumped out the back door like so much rubbish!

"Let's take a walk!" I say.

"Okay," Rich answers. We stroll around to the front of the church. Now it begins to dawn on me that no arrests are being made. Why? Not enough room for the bodies.

The lights of a TV camera blind my eyes.

"How about a statement?" shouts a voice from the darkness beyond the glare. I can see the outline of huge lenses reaching out to capture my response.

I square off and exclaim, "This is outrageous! It's unthinkable! Unbelievable! This is supposed to be the United

States of America — but this is the kind of thing that happens in Russia! Imagine it! A hundred men dragged out of a church while praying to their God, and dumped on the ground! I don't believe it!"

Good Morning America picked up a punch-line from this statement and ran it on national television. Lois saw it.

There is commotion as officers haul the last few men out. I see some officers standing around the double front doors, as if guarding them. Our men stand idly, looking over the scene.

"Who can start a song?" I shouted. "God *Save* America!"

Instantly a splendid voice peels out in the chilly predawn air. Right on key. The whole milling throng joins in at the second syllable and sings with rousing gusto: "God *save* America, land that I love. . . ."

Independent cameraman Jeff Harsh is still inside the building with the final remnants being cleared. He sees Sheriff Tesch gloating to some media people. Jeff walks up to the sheriff and hurls a challenge into his teeth.

"Tell me, Sheriff, how long do you suppose it will be before you'll be carrying these same people to the gas ovens?"

The furious sheriff darkens his brow toward Jeff.

"Who are you and what are you doing here?" the sheriff asks.

"I'm a free lance TV man," Jeff responds. "I travel around the country and shoot a lot of footage — but I've never seen anything quite like this. Let me ask you — how are you going to look your grandchildren in the face when you go home?"

"I have an order from the court!" blurts the agitated Tesch.

"Does that order suspend the Constitution of the United States?"

"I have to do my job!"

"Did you ever take an oath to uphold the Constitution of the United States?"

"Yes, I did!"

"Then why are you violating the First Amendment to that Constitution by depriving these people of their religious rights?"

Sheriff Fred Tesch is fed up. He's had all he can take.

"Throw this man out!" he rages. "He's one of *them!*"

Jeff looks straight into the eyes of the fuming sheriff.

"The only way I'm going out of here is feet first!" he says.

Sheriff's deputies grab Jeff Harsh, carry him out of the building and dump him.

Several officers are bunched up in front of the church doors.

"John 3:16 in unison!" I shout. "God so loved. . . ." The crowd of godly men split the low-hanging cloud cover with the Word of God.

Greg Dixon's indomitable spirit is not easily suppressed. Having been thrown out of the church, he watches for an opening. Seizing a moment when the officers are not looking, he walks back into the church and kneels again in prayer.

For a second time Greg is dumped out of the building by officers.

The incident makes top headline, front-page news back home in the *Indianapolis Star.*

"Jesus was carried into Jerusalem by *one* jackass," he is quoted as saying. "I was carried out of church by *four* of them!"

Dr. David Brown, seventy-five-year-old pastor of the Yakima Bible Baptist Church, Yakima, Washington, and editor of the *Western Messenger*, a well-built man of large physical stature, is the senior of all of us in terms of age. He has raced across the country to stand with us, arriving at Faith Baptist Church around 5:00 a.m.

Barely an hour later the officers have entered the church. With all 210 pounds of his weight the dignified Dr. Brown resists. Television footage is to show four officers fully engaged — one holding each leg and one holding each arm — struggling desperately to transport the man. They manage to dump him out of the church, but it costs them some extra muscle power and time. Dr. Brown makes his point!

Having evicted all of us, the sheriff stations four of his armed deputies inside the church, chains and padlocks the double glass front doors on the *inside*.

It is 6:30 a.m., and the dawn is delayed due to cloud cover. I stand in the outer lawn area comparing experiences with half a dozen other men. Suddenly the word "Pastor" is spoken softly just behind my right ear.

I turn to look level into the eyes of State Patrol Captain R. Syslo. He extends his right hand. Slowly mine reaches out and grasps it.

"How are you feeling, Captain?"

He utters no words, but his honest and compassionate visage speaks volumes to me. He's apparently too choked up to speak, but he's telling me he's sorry.

The pause is over. Releasing my hand, he turns to walk away. Instinctively I extend my left hand and pat him on the back, something like a man will stroke a good friend.

The human encounter touches me deeply. Emotion wells up from the core of my being. We are men of the same fiber — but we happen to be on opposite sides. I know he respects our cause and our convictions, as I respect his position.

Within a day or two the captain's wife will call our telephone center. She will convey admiration for our stand, and assure us of her prayers. Captain and Mrs. Syslo are good people. I'm planning to add them to my Christmas card list.

I recall the incident with a strong sense of disbelief. Never had I expected to see and experience the events of the early dark hours of October 18, 1982.

A dozen squad cars had converged at the small church. Eighteen officers had physically expelled a hundred men of God, taken possession of the church building, stationed armed guards on the inside, and chained and padlocked the premises.

Rushing across the country from meetings in Pennsylvania, Dr. Roy Thompson, pastor of the Cleveland Baptist Church, stops to check in by phone. He is told that a hundred men have been thrown out of the church, that the place has been chained and padlocked, and that armed deputies are now stationed inside.

"The news hit me like a volcano," Thompson reported later. "I couldn't believe it. I still don't believe it. This can't happen in America! We've got to put a stop to it!"

What happened in the pre-dawn hours of October 18 was but another skirmish in the long history of freedom. Although we were thrown out, we won the skirmish. Within a day and a half, victory was to be ours. We passed through the vale of humiliation for the cause of Christ, and God honored our stand.

Those who shared that moment are unified by a bond that will never be broken. There are those who will not understand. Some will judge us.

But none can deprive us of the deep satisfaction that is ours for having confronted state tyranny at the threshold. We belong to the steadfast remnant of the ages who refused to retreat. It was the strong and the brave who forged our freedoms — some in the fires of suffering, some by simply standing and looking tyranny in the face.

We will always be known as "A Hundred Who Stood."

3

Swamped in a Storm

"They that wait on the Lord
shall renew their strength . . ." (Isaiah 40:31).

October 18 is a day of regrouping. We are terribly fatigued, and we have lost our command post. The seven telephones in the church are no longer available to us. The convenience of a specially built van to serve as a mobile command post occurs to us. But we just don't have such a vehicle.

Perhaps to an outsider we look somewhat demoralized. We meet for a time at the home of Assistant Pastor Phil Schmidt. I inquire about rental of the American Legion hall in town.

"Nothing doing!" says the Legion contact. "You guys have caused too much trouble around this town!"

"A prophet is not without honor except in his own country," said Jesus. This principle was never demonstrated more strikingly than here in Louisville.

Pastor Sileven should be acclaimed and heroized by his hometown. Instead, he is despised and villified. The people of Louisville regard Sileven as a "lawbreaker," little realiz-

24

ing it's the state of Nebraska that is preeminently deserving of that shameful distinction.

Throughout the long history of the struggle for freedom on this planet, it's the Silevens who have gone to the wall for the ungrateful crowd. The Sileven types have ever been scorned by those who have benefited the most.

Boiling up in my being is a desire to pen some kind of epistle titled "To Louisville." Jesus pronounced judgments against cities of His day that spurned the light of God. The fiery prophets of the Old Testament era had done likewise.

The kind folks and gentle people of Louisville would rather go straight to hell than listen to one syllable of God's truth through the mouth of the prophet of God who dwells among them. They would sooner listen to the hateful likes of the degenerate and malicious sheriff who struts among them.

My prayer is that God will have mercy on them.

"He that is not for me is against me," said Jesus. Those who are against Jesus' people are against Jesus.

I walk outside of Phil Schmidt's home and find myself talking to a Channel 7 camera crew. They wonder what we're going to do now.

"We've lost a little skirmish," I tell them, "but not the war. We need some rest and then we'll regroup to decide on our next move."

I linger to teach the camera crew a lesson on freedom and what makes it happen.

"We're on the winning side," I assure them. "We'll win this struggle."

An optimistic assessment, to say the least! For nearly six years Faith Baptist Church has had to fall back before the relentless encroachment of state tyranny. All legal recourse has failed. Now the pastor is in jail. A hundred

men who came to make a stand for the pastor and his principles have been ejected from the church bodily. The
church building and the day school facility which it houses
are chained and padlocked. Armed guards occupy the
premises.

It looks very much like total defeat. But not a man of
our number will accept defeat. That word is not in our
vocabulary.

Suddenly I recall that the Word says:

> *They that wait on the Lord shall renew their
> strength. They shall mount up with wings as eagles.
> They shall run and not be weary. They shall walk and
> not faint.*

A stillness creeps over Louisville in the middle of the
day as the soldiers of Christ disappear. The place becomes
a ghost town.

Back at our motels we tumble into bed for four solid
hours. We awake refreshed and ready to take on the
world.

Meanwhile a storm has rolled in from the North and bliz-
zard winds are driving damp snow at an almost horizontal
angle. Temperatures have plunged below freezing.

In this crazy war, we, the forces of constitutional
freedom, asked no mercy when the emissaries of state
tyranny came for us. Now we offer no mercy.

The church authorities call the power company and
order the electrical service cut off. The church quickly
turns into a refrigerator — and the officers stationed
within can no longer stand the bone-rending chill. Some-
time during the night they vacate the place, leaving it still
chained and padlocked. We contemplate cutting the chain
now — but conclude that it's not yet the right time.

Greg Dixon and I occupy room 244 at the Ben Franklin Motel, ten miles from Louisville beside the intersection of highways 50 and 80. This austere room, furnished with two queen-sized beds and one telephone, now serves as the only command post we have.

Beginning around mid-afternoon the phone starts ringing off the hook. Alarmed at the morning television news coverage showing our men being dragged out of the church and dumped into the darkness, men of God are calling in from everywhere. They're coming to join in the battle with us. Some are already arriving. Now they burst into our room, full of spiritual power and physical vigor. They are alarmed and ready for battle. Fresh troops! What an encouragement to those of us who have seen little sleep since Saturday night!

Dr. Roy Thompson, pastor of the 6,000-member Cleveland Baptist Church, has sped across the states from his meetings in Philadelphia. He is a prince among men. Handsome, resolute, tough — he is committed to Christ without reservation. His arrival is a great encouragement.

The congregation of Faith Baptist Church has elected him principal of its school and has elected me vice-principal to serve with him. Roy Thompson is destined to occupy a very important leadership role at the very vanguard of the fray that looms ominously ahead.

Pastor Bud Ammerman now comes to our rescue. He makes the facilities of nearby Marshall Drive Baptist Church available to us for an evening strategy meeting and rally. Fourteen of us meet in a back room to plan strategy while the crowd gathers and begins singing in the auditorium.

Quickly we structure our basic organization. We set up seven task forces, each with a leader chosen for demonstrated boldness and ability, including the following:

Legal Task Force: Bob McCurry and Bob Muncaster

Communications: Greg Dixon, Ed Rowe and Ken Haney

Political Action: Ed Thibadeaux, Bill Laurent, Harry Jackson, Dr. Simon, Tom Corkish, Bruce Gorter, Brothers Cantrell and Davidson

Preacher Calling: Many men

Vehicles and Transportation: Ron Tottingham, an excellent man who once saw heavy combat in a hot shooting war in Vietnam.

Scheduling: Bob Folger

Crisis Management: Clay Nuttall and Buddy Gillespie, joined by many others.

The slogan of this new organized effort is "A Job for Every Volunteer."

Pastor Richard Moore is general operational coordinator.

The strategy group enters the auditorium at 9:45 p.m. The music of heaven raises the rafters. Our ranks have swollen. Only this morning a hundred of us were thrown out of the church. Now at least two hundred and fifty men stand before us. Each man is as dedicated as any of us who were ejected. It is a beautiful sight.

The crowd is seized with the assured spirit of victory. We are God's men. Let every devil, every tyrant, every imp of hell tremble. God is greater than all, and He indwells us in the Person of His Holy Spirit.

We had been swamped in a storm. Yet more hundreds of God's people are rushing to our side. Soon it will be the forces of tyranny that will be swamped in the storm. Not a man doubts it.

Victory will be ours.

4

Point of No Retreat

"I gave my legs in Vietnam for a cause that was less important than the freedom to serve Christ. I'm ready to give my life if necessary . . ." (Evangelist Tim Lee).

It is Tuesday, October 19. Our phone bank swings into action. Scores of men call pastor friends and acquaintances in other parts of the nation, and urge them to hasten to Louisville. Already many are en route. Others respond affirmatively on the spot.

By last evening, some two hundred and fifty men have arrived at the scene of battle. By tonight our ranks swell to about six hundred. By tomorrow night our number will have burgeoned to approximately one thousand men of God.

All of these men have taken emergency leave of their busy ministries. They have rushed from approximately thirty states to stand with Pastor Sileven. These modern minutemen are valiant heroes of the faith and guardians of our American freedoms.

Millions of sleepy citizens of this beleaguered land who are blissfully unaware of the contemporary challenge to our freedoms should rise up and call them blessed.

Indeed there comes powerfully to my mind a steadfast conclusion that if there is any hope for America at all, it lies in tens of thousands of men of the pulpit, fully supported by their churches, who will rush to every remote crossroads where constitutional liberty is in jeopardy and stand.

We live in a time in which legal brushfires are flaming up suddenly, ominously, in diverse parts of the land. The epochal events which transpired in Louisville during the week of October 18, 1982, provide a strong basis for hope that our constitutional liberties can be preserved if the leaders of God's people will but pay the price.

In order to enable the reader to experience the events of these crisis days with me, I capture them in the present tense for the printed page, working from notes jotted in my ever-present writing tablet, and from a memory rendered vivid by the drama of the events themselves.

Evangelist Tim Lee has interrupted services in California and flown in to take part in the battle of Louisville. Tim is a splendid specimen of humanity. He is handsome in his Marine Corps dress uniform. He paid a horrible price for his service in Vietnam, having lost both legs in combat. From his wheelchair, Tim delivers some of the most powerful messages heard anywhere in the nation these days.

Upon arrival on the scene of action in this different kind of war in Louisville, Tim leaves no doubt as to his commitment.

"I went ten thousand miles and gave my legs for a cause that was less important than this one. I'm ready to give my life, if necessary, for the far greater cause of freedom to serve Christ. I feel like getting a pair of chain cutters and cutting that chain, then going in there and holding a revival meeting," he says.

A remarkable change is taking place in the press and media coverage of the Battle of Louisville. John Whitesides, *Omaha World-Herald* staff writer, is contributing excellent front-page write-ups on a daily basis. His work is in contrast to the editorial position of the same paper, which is obviously hostile.

Numerous men among us are getting the word out through radio talk shows back in their home towns. Twice I appear on the Moody Radio Network with Jim Warren and Melinda Correa. Barbara Studley of WNWS-Miami, opens her lines to share my special report with the largest talk-show audience in Florida.

Jeff Harsh introduces me by telephone to Kathy Osbeck of CBN and I arrange to have Jeff's video footage forwarded to our Coral Ridge Ministries studio in Fort Lauderdale for program planning assessment. Pat Robertson updates his national audience daily, and generates a hundred thousand calls to the White House.

The *Indianapolis Star* carries daily front-page coverage with a focus on the leadership and experience of Dr. Greg Dixon in the Louisville fray.

ABC's *Good Morning America* and Cable Network News cover the incident. Gradually the truth is seeping out to the nation. Everywhere people respond with shock, amazement, even tears. The typical response: "This can't happen in America!"

The towering stature of Pastor Lester Roloff of Corpus Christi is known to all. His personal appearance for a couple of hours with us provides valuable perspective.

"It cost us a million dollars to fight off the forces of state tyranny in Texas," he reports. "The struggle lasted eight years. God gave us victory with respect. Every godly candidate in Texas has eaten at my table this year. I enjoy the respect and friendship of the governor. Some people are referring to me as the most powerful political figure in Texas these days."

Asked for his assessment of the current Louisville situation, Dr. Roloff was decisive.

"When the authorities of the state of Nebraska threw you men out of the church, they made themselves liable. They went too far. If you conduct yourselves right from this point on, you can win with respect. Already you have much greater support than I did when I took my stand," he says.

The issue in Texas had been similar to the present one in Nebraska. The state of Texas had moved in to require the licensing of religion. Caesar had attempted to usurp the role of Christ.

Roloff sensed the dire implications of the state initiative.

"When I take a license from the state to do the work of Christ," vowed Roloff, "I'll throw my Bible in the first garbage can I can find."

Lester Roloff stood and fought. He won not only the war but the respect of his fellow Texas citizens as well.

Out of Roloff's stand there has come leadership for Louisville. Out of Louisville will arise leadership for other confrontations. There are strategy discussions about the formation of a rapid-response national capability to pounce decisively on any brushfire that might threaten our legitimate constitutional freedoms anywhere in the nation. I believe God is fashioning the spearhead of a movement that might well have the potential of turning this nation around.

A wise man of the past generation is quoted as having stated, "There will come a time in America when we Christians will reach a point from which we cannot retreat."

The collective sense of the stalwart men of God who have gathered to Louisville is that the prediction is being fulfilled. That time of no retreat has arrived. The time is now. The wall is behind us, and we look the enemy in the face. Someone will retreat . . . and it will not be us.

For the second consecutive evening we meet for strategy planning and a rousing rally at Marshall Drive Baptist Church. A potent strategy, developed in embryonic form yesterday, is expanded. Things are coming together splendidly. Enthusiasm is growing. There is singing and praying.

Evangelist Tim Lee is introduced. The pulpit is set to one side and Tim sits on the platform in his wheelchair, facing the audience.

Tim quotes the First Amendment and comments: "The government has no business meddling with the church. Why, the government can't even handle its *own* business!"

The six hundred men explode with applause and cheering.

Tim lays it on.

"Who would have believed, twenty years ago, that a preacher who loves God, who loves the Bible, and who loves children, would be sitting in a jail house? God never called the government to educate your children. The bureaucrats are moving in and trying to take over the ministry of Christ!"

We assess the situation. We believe Sheriff Tesch and County Prosecutor Ronald Moravec are between a rock and a hard place. That's just where we want them. Our aggressive and confrontive style will wear them out. Already they are swamped with phone calls. They haven't seen anything yet! Neither has Judge Case.

A decision is made that we will hold a giant rally tomorrow in Plattsmouth. We will begin the event at 11:30 a.m. in the facility of the First Baptist Church of Plattsmouth. Then we will walk the half-mile to the county jail where we will rally on the steps and upper landing that leads to the entrance. We will proceed the twelve miles to Louisville by car caravan, where we will cut the chain at 3:00 p.m., enter Faith Baptist Church and hold a meeting.

Tim Lee came all the way from California to cut that chain. Our plan for the cutting will be to rally outside the church. A pair of long-handled bolt cutters will be handed to Tim. Some of us will accompany Tim's wheelchair as he rolls it up to the double glass doors at the main entrance.

Through the doors we will speak to the officers inside and tell them what we are going to do. We will assure them that if they will simply stand back, they will not be harmed. If their revolvers come out and they threaten our lives, Tim will proceed to cut the chain anyway. There will be no turning back from our goal. The state has no right to occupy and chain the church. If they shoot us, it will be *their* problem!

Someone rushes in with a question. "Several buses are coming from Illinois tomorrow. One is bringing a Christian high school civics class. Is that okay?"

"Absolutely!" says Greg Dixon. "They'll get a lesson in civics . . . and also a lesson in *history!* Let them come along."

Word comes in that the American Civil Liberties Union (ACLU) believes we have a hot civil rights case against Nebraska for throwing us out of the church yesterday. In fact, the ACLU wants to handle the case for us. It would be a feather in their cap. But there is no way that we would even think of turning to such a far-out left wing outfit for help.

It has been a good day. Men of God still roll in from all over America. The planning for tomorrow proceeds well past midnight. Greg, Roy, Rich Moore, Bob McCurry, Richard Angwin and I finalize the details in 244. It is past 1:00 a.m. before we retire.

"Lord, enable me to unwind and relax. Give me restful sleep. Re-energize my body for the day ahead. I belong to You. Uphold Your cause and manifest Your glory through me, unworthy as I am. Guide my feet into paths of righteousness. Bless all these men and the dear ones back home who stand behind them. Shake America to her senses," I pray.

5

Justice and the Judge

*"Power corrupts — and absolute power
corrupts absolutely" (Lord Acton).*

Nebraska's District Judge Raymond J. Case was the
unhappy recipient of a powerful and accusatory "Open
Letter" that I shot his way on September 5, in the wake of
the jailing of Pastor Everett Sileven. In the Divine Providence a combination of unpredictable circumstances led
our paths together late on the morning of Wednesday, October 20, 1982.

To chronicle the experiences of the judge's life that
shaped his judicial values and impelled him to sign court
orders jailing Pastor Everett Sileven and padlocking his
church would be an impossible task. The focus of this
writing is the plain fact that this happened; not *why* it happened.

It is a fast-moving Wednesday, and one that is destined
to gain a notable place in the annals of Faith Baptist
Church's six-year struggle for rights that have properly
belonged to it and to all churches ever since our constitutional government was declared in effect on March 4,

1789.

Upon arising this morning, Dr. Greg Dixon and I have prayer. During this time of prayer both of us are strongly impressed that we must make an effort to see Judge Case personally. The judge is reached by telephone, and agrees to see us.

Before 10:30 a.m. Dr. Roy Thompson, Dr. Greg Dixon and I are in a spacious carpeted van provided by one of the young ministers. We swivel our seats around so that we are meeting around the table, conference style, while the youthful preacher presses the accelerator to the legal limit as we speed toward Nebraska City — some fifty miles away.

In the course of the conversation Roy Thompson suggests the wisdom of a "Declaration of Religious Liberty."

We chat about this for a few moments, and words begin to come. I open the black-covered case that contains my writing tablet and begin to write:

"We, the signers of this Declaration, hereby pledge our lives, our possessions, and our sacred honor to return America to the biblical and constitutional foundation of her religious, civic and governmental freedoms.

"We pledge our primary allegiance to almighty God and to no other. We will not bow to any government that would impose a reign of tyranny over biblically based religious conscience.

"To the extent that the laws and leadership of our beloved America adhere to her founding principles as immortalized in our Constitution, we will be loyal citizens. To the extent that America denies her God, persecutes the people of God, and tramples her own Constitution, we will oppose her at the threshold.

"We will not yield up the minds and souls of our

children to a godless state. We will not sacrifice our principles on the altar of expediency. We will not be restrained from recognizing God within all areas of the life of America. We will proclaim the Word of God freely throughout the whole range of the institutional life of this nation.

"If we are jailed for the performance of righteousness, we will proclaim the salvation of Jesus Christ boldly to every warden, to every guard, to every inmate."

Thus the brief initial draft of the Declaration is penned. In due course it will be expanded, published separately and circulated among our congregations. I believe God will use it to weld the minds and souls of many thousands of His people together for the preservation of freedom.

It is 11:20 a.m. when our van pulls to the curb in front of the courthouse in Nebraska City. Quickly Roy, Greg and I step out and move briskly up the paved walkway toward the main entrance to the classical-style old midwestern building.

Momentarily we pause to read the inscription that is carved in granite over the door: "May all who suffer injustice find their habitation here."

But the court system has failed us. It has ignored our Constitution, jailed a godly pastor and locked up his church. Now, three men of God enter a place that claims to protect people from injustice. We believe it has become a citadel of *injustice*, and we come to represent the God of all true justice. In the impending clash between man's injustice and God's justice, what will happen? We have no weapons, no worldly authority, no legal tricks.

We advance as men clothed with the armor of God. We wear the belt of truth, the breastplate of righteousness and the helmet of salvation. We carry the shield of faith and we wield the Sword of the Spirit, which is the Word of God.

By this time eight hundred men of God are on their knees in the First Baptist Church of Plattsmouth praying for the will of God to be accomplished as we meet with Judge Case. We pass through the inner corridor and upstairs toward the office of the judge, fully cognizant that the weapons of our warfare are not carnal, but mighty through God to the pulling down of strongholds. . . .

At the top of the courthouse stairway we start looking for the judge's office. Greg and Roy disappear into a side room to the right to make inquiry. I cover the left side of the corridor and presently, through an open doorway, I see a grey-haired man wearing spectacles and a few facial wrinkles. He sees me, rises from the desk where he has been working, and walks toward me.

"Judge Case?"

"Yes," he says mildly, extending his hand.

Roy and Greg step into the corridor and I introduce them to Judge Case.

"Let's go in here and meet at the conference table," says the judge pointing to the end of the corridor. We walk along the corridor with him and into the courtroom. He motions for us to be seated at the huge conference table.

I scrutinize the features of the man who, as far as I know, has perpetrated immense wrongs against Pastor Sileven and Faith Baptist Church. The man before me appears too mild to be a deliberate persecutor of good people. I wonder if he has been impelled by pressures that are beyond my understanding, given the limited data available to me.

Judge Case looks tired, worn, bedraggled. He has been receiving telephone calls from everywhere, he says, and the one matter that concerns us has occupied most of his time for a number of days. He's been in a whirlwind of meetings. I see him as a man at wit's end.

Roy Thompson, acting principal of Faith Christian School, wades in directly.

"There's only one church in America that's chained and padlocked," he begins, "and that's Faith Baptist Church. We think it's deplorable, and something needs to be done about it."

"I've been thinking about a possible solution," replies Judge Case. "Would you consider moving the school across the Cass County line to another location?"

"That wouldn't solve anything," says Roy Thompson. "The same Nebraska laws are in effect in the neighboring county. They could launch an action over there, just like Cass County did. Besides, that school is a ministry of Faith Baptist Church. It is inseparable from the church. Where the church is, the school is. There's something terribly wrong about moving any part of the ministry of that church, when it already has a suitable location."

Roy touched on the central issue distinguishing our viewpoint from that of the state of Nebraska. Pastor Sileven and all who stand with him believe very strongly in the *inseparability* of church and school, within the framework of biblical faith and practice. The state of Nebraska and its court system believe in the *separability* of church and school. To them a church is a church and a school is a school. They do not admit any validity to our viewpoint whatever.

Throughout the two hours and forty minutes that we spend with Judge Case on October 20, it is apparent that he does not comprehend this fundamental distinction. Again and again his remarks indicate to us that such a view is foreign to his understanding. Time and again we object to one expression or another from the judge that demonstrates clearly his failure to recognize our position.

"Your statement proves you don't grasp our true position," we tell him repeatedly. In desperation I make one final attempt to convey our point.

"Your Honor, it might well be that this concept is foreign to your religious faith (Judge Case identified himself as a Catholic). Perhaps that's why you don't see it as we see it. But it seems to me that you're responsible to recognize the existence of the deeply held religious convictions of others, even though you might not share them yourself," I explain to him.

Greg Dixon cites the sixth chapter of Deuteronomy and other scripture passages in an attempt to support our position. Eventually, after returning to this key consideration numerous times, I begin to believe the judge understands that it is truly an article of faith with us. Although he does not voice his understanding, his responses begin to sound as if he perceives the essence of our position.

Relentlessly we press our position, in the face of Judge Case's repeated references to the Nebraska Supreme Court and its action in upholding his own decisions. I reach for my pocket-sized edition of the Declaration of Independence, the Bill of Rights and the United States Constitution, published by the American Legion. Holding it in my hand, I quote from memory the religious liberty portion of the First Amendment: "Congress shall make no law respecting an establishment of religion, or prohibiting the free exercise thereof. . . ."

The judge asks if he may take a look at it. I slide the document across the immense conference table to him. He picks it up and appears to adjust his eyes to the text, then reads it haltingly.

Greg Dixon later remarks that Judge Case acted as if he

had not read the First Amendment for twenty-five years!

"We're just simple folks," I tell the judge. "Our reading of this First Amendment leaves no room for any kind of governmental regulation of religion whatever. It states clearly that government cannot make any laws which prohibit the free exercise of religion. It seems to us that the jailing of a pastor, the locking of his church, and the stationing of armed guards inside it, involves a clear prohibition of the free exercise of religion. These actions are just simply unconstitutional, since no other offense than the practice of the pastor's religious faith is involved."

"But the Supreme Court of Nebraska has upheld the case against Faith Baptist Church," replies Judge Case.

I now ask the key question: "Your Honor, did you take an oath of office to uphold the United States Constitution?"

"Yes, I did."

"Then it seems to me that's exactly what you ought to do, under any and all circumstances. When the time comes that you and your court will stand tall and make your decisions on the basis of the Constitution, regardless of the viewpoint or decisions of any other court, you can hardly imagine how many friends you'll have. If the Nebraska Supreme Court wants to overrule you, that's their problem, not yours. Our effort in that case would be directed toward them and not toward you," I tell him.

The issue to which some legal authorities refer as "interpretivism" is paramount in this discussion. Is the United States Constitution a document to be *believed* at face value, or *interpreted* away?

I ask the judge whether he has ever read the written

Constitution of Russia. He replies that he has not.

"I have read it," I inform him, "and it contains a very fine statement guaranteeing freedom of religion."

I discern a degree of surprise in the countenance of the judge.

"You see, it's one thing to have a good Constitution, and quite another thing to be guided by it. Russia's constitutional freedom-of-religion ideal is floating around somewhere up in the clouds. Down at the level of reality, they send their preachers to Siberian concentration camps for crimes like distributing the scriptures or teaching children on the streets about Jesus. The written contents of a Constitution are not worth the paper they're printed on unless they are vigorously applied by judges like yourself.

"There is an ever-present danger that the gap between our own constitutional ideal and grass roots reality will become wider and wider — until our entire nation passes under a kind of judicial rule that is far astray from the Constitution. The American people can't allow that to happen. It is the road to tyranny," I explain.

Judge Case listens attentively. I have a feeling that he respects what we say. He does not appear to be in the mood for verbal combat. But my reference to "tyranny" reminds him of the open letter I had directed to him on September 5.

"That letter you wrote was vitriolic," he comments.

"I wrote it in the wake of your court order that put Dr. Sileven in jail," I reply. "The situation called for a strong letter, and I wrote it. What happened there was unthinkable, unbelievable. I was angry about such a miscarriage of justice. I still am. But I will review that letter when I get an opportunity to do so, and if I feel that I owe you an apology for anything in it, I'll certainly convey an apology to you."

I have since reviewed my open letter of September 5, and I find in it nothing to apologize about. Yes, it is a strong letter. But the rape of our constitutional freedoms must call forth the strongest of communications and the most resolute of actions. Otherwise our freedoms will soon be consumed as dry stubble before a prairie fire.

While we are on the subject of tyranny, I take the opportunity to tell the judge how I feel about Sheriff Fred Tesch.

"There is a tyrant mentality if I ever encountered one," I observe. "The man readily goes into a rage at the slightest provocation. Personally, I don't feel like he's a fit man to be wearing a gun."

Roy and Greg both back me up in this assessment, and Roy takes a swipe at Cass County Prosecutor Ronald Moravec.

"That guy keeps coming up with demands that you make these tough moves against a man of God and a school that's doing a far better job than the public schools," Roy accuses. "He's bad news, and the worst thing about it is that he and Sheriff Tesch are both doing their best to use you as a tool to accomplish their designs!"

Greg Dixon and Roy Thompson get into the intricacies of some legal cases involving situations similar to Nebraska's case against Sileven. They make reference to the Whisner case, and to Yoder vs. Wisconsin.

Judge Case makes notes on the pad in front of him.

The churches pastored by Roy and Greg both operate large Christian schools. They have had to stand their ground and fight off the bureaucratic wolves. They speak out of experience, and their acquaintance with other relevant cases lends weight to their conviction.

In the eternal fight for freedom, the battle goes to the strong. Not to the physically strong, but always to the spiritually strong. I find myself praising God, under my breath, for Roy and Greg. Where would the nation be without men like them?

Tyranny is by nature aggressive. Like a giant, voracious bear, it moves relentlessly through time intimidating all who fear. Corruption in high places stalks the corridors of history, devouring the innocent.

"Power corrupts," exclaimed Lord Acton, "and absolute power corrupts absolutely."

This is precisely the problem in Nebraska — and God has graciously raised up Greg and Roy and well over a thousand other strong warriors of the faith.

In the providence of God it has fallen our lot to stand in the gap and stop the rising flood-tide that threatens to overwhelm our civilization. The spirit of tyranny is abroad in the land. Sheriff Tesch and Prosecutor Moravec are only pawns in a larger conspiracy of evil. We are the expendables — the people who are ready to give our all, if necessary, in order to turn back the tide.

Like the few Spartans who stood in the press at Thermopylae in 480 B.C. and held off the Persian legions of Xerxes, we stand in the gap. We occupy the point at which the enslaving forces of humanist tyranny and the liberating forces of Divine righteousness meet. Their ill-framed "laws" that ignore constitutional values are backed up by courts and jails and guns. We face them with nothing in our hand but the Sword of the Spirit . . . and we do not blink.

"Lord, please send more of Your people to our side. Many, many more of the strong and the brave. Raise up churches that will stand ready to send their pastor off to the war at a moment's notice. Marshall the spiritual resources that are needed to win the day for righteousness. Glorify Your Name through Your people," I pray.

In the course of our meeting with Judge Case, he mentions a very important passage of scripture.

"A minister called me this morning," says Case, "and voiced his total support for the position I've been taking. He said he's basing his support on Romans 13, which instructs people to obey the authorities."

"Let me show you just what Romans 13 teaches," counters Greg Dixon, flipping his Bible open instantly to that chapter.

With the skill of a seasoned surgeon, Greg proceeds to expound the message of this great chapter to the attentive judge.

"Rulers are not a terror to good works, but to the evil," Greg stresses from verse three. He goes on to press the unique role of the civic authority as "the minister of God" to the people "for good."

In the most masterful way, Greg drives home his point.

"Judge Case, you are a minister of God in the civic realm. You have awesome powers . . ." he says.

"I know," interjects the judge. "I am aware of that. And I also know that I am only a man and I can make mistakes just like anyone else."

The judge says this humbly, sincerely. I study his features. I seem to see integrity there. I wonder what God sees.

Greg continues to expound the scriptures. He lacks no words.

"Whoever called to pledge his support for your position on the basis of Romans 13 just doesn't know the meaning of this passage. If he were knowledgeable about the scriptures, he would hold you responsible for jailing a man of God for the performance of *good* works. He would notice in verse three that you are not supposed to bring judgment against a man for good works. He would see in verse four that you are actually a minister of God to people for *good*, and that you should only execute wrath against those who do *evil*. On the basis of this scripture it is clear that Everett Sileven should never have been sent to jail and that his church never should have been chained and padlocked!" he explains.

Judge Case listens intently, but offers no verbal response.

He requests our addresses. "I might want to write to you men some day," he says just above a whisper.

I slide my card across the table to him. Judge Case looks at it, then looks right at me and speaks words that amaze me. "I listen to Dr. Kennedy every Sunday."

"Yes," I respond, "and what Kennedy is that?"

"The one from Fort Lauderdale. Dr. James Kennedy. I hear his radio sermon from Coral Ridge Ministries every Sunday," he says.

I find myself amazed almost beyond belief. The judge has, in the course of the conversation, identified himself as a Roman Catholic. Now he informs me that he is a faithful listener to Dr. Kennedy's broadcast, produced by Coral Ridge Ministries, which I am serving as Executive Director! And here I am, a representative of the same Dr. Kennedy, in a heavy confrontation with the judge that has already lasted two and a half hours! What a strange world!

Meanwhile our big rally is in progress at the jail, forty miles away in Plattsmouth.

"I hear men singing outside," writes Pastor Sileven in a

note to his wife, Tressie, which he dates 12:30 p.m. The music of heaven has penetrated the prison walls and filtered into his jail cell.

Pastor Larry Lautaret of the First Church of God in Kearney, Nebraska, is a man of handsome face and stout heart. At the earlier rally in the same location on September 3, following the jailing of Sileven, he had stood up on the jailhouse landing and delivered a soul-stirring message based on the second Psalm. Many of the men had remarked about the power of Larry's words.

Throughout the long days and nights of this struggle in September, and now in October, this choice man of God stays in the ranks. He was among the "Hundred Who Stood" and were bodily thrown out of the church in the pre-dawn moments of Monday. Now, at the request of Dr. Dixon voiced this morning before departing for Nebraska City, Larry Lautaret stands again on the jailhouse landing.

The Word of God falls as hammer blows from his eloquent lips, to the shouts and cheers of a thousand men of God. I shall always remember Larry Lautaret. He is a choice General of the King in this war for the freedom of God's people. The aroma of heaven accompanies him, and earth is richer because he serves among us.

Four times Greg, Roy and I make a move to leave Judge Case. We explain that we must get back to join our rally in Plattsmouth, and to hold our meeting in Faith Baptist Church. The judge appears puzzled, because he knows very well that the church is locked and guarded by armed men.

"Come on," exclaims the bewildered judge, "don't tell me you're going out there and pull that door down!"

"We didn't say that," Roy assures. "We just said we are going to have a meeting in that church this afternoon. If we end up in a pool of blood in front of that door, we're going to have a meeting in that church at three o'clock!"

"Your honor," I explain, "We realize your order allows the church to be unlocked by the sheriff at 5:00 p.m. for an evening meeting. But we've decided to meet inside the church at 3:00 p.m. It's a bit cold outside, you know."

We make no hint about our plans for Evangelist Tim Lee to roll up to the door in his wheelchair and cut the chain. There is a moment of tense silence as Judge Case studies our faces, his eyes shifting from one of us to another, then the other, then back again. We are not smiling. He knows we mean business. He knows he is looking at three men who are not bluffing.

"For almost three hours we've been waiting for you to ask us what we want, your Honor, and I haven't heard you ask it yet," I say.

"All right, I'll ask it now. Tell me what you want," he replies.

"We want Pastor Sileven out of jail and his church unchained permanently," I demand.

Again Judge Case pauses reflectively.

"Well, all right, come on," the judge says.

He rises, gestures with his hand, and we follow him from the room. Around the corner to the left we follow him, then into his inner office where he motions for us to sit down. He takes his place at his desk, picks up the phone and calls the office of Sheriff Tesch.

"Go ahead and unlock Faith Baptist Church right away," he tells the sheriff.

Now the judge looks at us.

"Give me a few hours. I need to talk with Charlie Craze (Sileven's counsel) and reflect on what can be done," he says.

We shake hands with Judge Raymond J. Case, walk hastily to our waiting van, and hit the road for Louisville, fifty miles away.

At exactly 2:57 p.m. I walk into Faith Baptist Church. Chains and locks have been removed by a deputy sheriff prior to our arrival. It would be impossible to describe my feelings as I enter the church auditorium and walk down the center aisle toward the platform. This is the hallowed ground we've been fighting for — and God has delivered it back to us. Exhilaration throbs in my breast.

Greg makes a press statement. Soon the multitudes come pouring in from Plattsmouth by automobile caravan. The men enter cheering and praising God. The crowd swells into the evening. The press and media people come in droves. There are video cameras everywhere. Standing room only! The platform is draped with human flesh. Overflow speakers are installed so that hundreds of people, packed in every downstairs room and in every hallway, can hear.

The air is charged. Spontaneously a thousand voices break out in singing. It's the same song that the smaller crowd (about seventy) sang on September 3 as Sheriff Fred Tesch arrested Pastor Sileven and escorted him to his waiting squad car.

> *I heard an old, old story,*
> *How a Savior came from glory.*
> *How He gave His life on Calvary*
> *To save a wretch like me.*
>
> *I heard about His groaning,*
> *Of His precious blood's atoning.*
> *Then I repented of my sins,*
> *And won the victory.*

O victory in Jesus, my Savior forever.
He sought me and bought me,
With His redeeming blood.
He loved me ere I knew Him,
And all my love is due Him.
He plunged me to victory,
Beneath the cleansing flood.

I heard about the mansion,
He has built for me in glory.
And I heard about the streets of gold,
Beyond the crystal sea.

About the angels singing,
And the old redemption story.
And some sweet day I'll sing up there
The song of victory.

O victory in Jesus, my Savior forever,
He sought me . . .

The building pulsates with the song of victory. Greg reports on the meeting with Judge Case. Roy introduces Tim Lee, whose spellbinding message strikes a responsive chord in the cheering audience.

Arthur Blessitt relates his experiences in the war for freedom to preach the saving power of Jesus.

I read the first draft of the Declaration of Religious Liberty.

Dr. D. James Kennedy suggests to the Presbytery of Southern Florida that a mailgram be sent to Louisville, and that a messenger be sent to represent the Presbytery and to read the mailgram.

Dr. David Todd, one of the pastors, proceeds to Louisville and reads the following message to this large rally:

10/19/82 Mailgram was sent:

Faith Baptist Church
Attn.: Pastor, Deacons and Congregation
Louisville, NE 68037

An open letter to: The pastor, deacons and congregation of the Faith Baptist Church, Louisville, Nebraska.

The Presbytery of Southern Florida of the Presbyterian Church in America expresses to you our love and sympathy in this critical time for you and the Church of Jesus Christ in America, and indeed, all those who love religious liberty. We are following with great interest and grave concern the appalling developments in the town of Louisville, which represent a very dark page in the history of religious liberty in America.

Our forefathers came to these shores to escape this sort of state persecution. The entire nation is aware of this persecution and is alarmed at the dangers which it portends for all religious liberty. We see this as an attack on the most fundamental of our liberties, that liberty which was first enumerated in the Bill of Rights and which is the foundation of all of our other liberties.

May God grant you the courage to stand in this hour of your trial.

Ralph Mittendorf
Stated Clerk of Presbytery of Southern Florida

Collins D. Weeber, Moderator of Presbytery of Southern Florida

While the rally is in progress a reporter has been shadowing Judge Case. The judge knows that, having occupied the church building, we will not leave voluntarily. Also, he has received reports about the size of the crowd.

Sheriff Tesch wants to tear gas us out of the building, just as he had wanted to do on Monday.

Captain Syslo will have nothing to do with tear gassing us, and he makes it clear that he will not even have anything to do with carrying the bodies of men of God out of the building this time. Captain Syslo calls Governor Charles Thone, who agrees with his viewpoint and backs him all the way.

Under these circumstances, Judge Case issues a court order suspending indefinitely the previous order to keep the church chained and locked except for Wednesday nights and weekends when regular services are held. The reporter who has covered the judge grabs a copy of the court order and rushes it the twelve miles from Plattsmouth to Louisville.

At the height of our rally, Greg holds the document in the air and shouts, "Here's a court order from Judge Case. It says the church will not be locked any more, and we will not be thrown out!"

Never have I heard such ear-splitting cheers and praises to God!

Victory is sweet.

A day and a half later Pastor Sileven is brought from his jail cell to Judge Case's court. There ensues a bitter exchange between Prosecutor Moravec and the judge. Moravec is adamantly opposed to any thought of releasing the pastor.

At one point the judge raises his voice from the high bench and asserts, "These people have some constitutional rights!"

With that, he releases Pastor Sileven in spite of the raging hostility of Sheriff Tesch and Prosecutor Moravec.

On Friday evening, October 22, Pastor Everett Sileven is literally carried in triumph into Faith Baptist Church, on the shoulders of victorious supporters. The press and media of the nation are present. The national networks and the independents capture the moment, but no reporting does justice to the occasion.

The atmosphere is literally charged as some twelve hundred people pack into a place that normally seats two hundred and fifty. Great speeches are made to the ear-splitting cheers of the throng. The crowd explodes as Everett Sileven, pastor of Faith Baptist Church and defender of religious freedom, stands again in his pulpit and addresses the audience.

Will truth remain forever on the scaffold, and wrong forever on the throne? No, the nightmarish scenario painted by the pessimistic poet does not represent the shape of the future. Victories already granted reassure us that God will put wrong on the scaffold and truth on the throne.

After a fight of nearly six years, defeat mocked a little church in Nebraska. Its pastor was in jail and its building was chained and padlocked.

Then, in five short days, all of that changed. God's people gathered to the sound of the bugle. We went into action. And we went to see the judge. We told him about constitutional justice, about righteousness and judgment.

One of the lawyers summed up the outcome.

"In less than three hours, three men of God accomplished more by talking to the judge than our legal approach had accomplished in five years!"

Victory! Yes, but only a temporary one at best. The continuing war between the forces of freedom and state tyranny rages on.

6

Victory Will Come

"And he that sat upon the throne said,
Behold, I make all things new" (Revelation 21:5).

A valiant man of God paid a short visit to the front during the battle of Louisville. Pastors and others who had been dumped out of the church gathered outside the locked building to hear our brother in Christ, Lester Roloff. I switched on my Lanier recorder and picked up his brief remarks.

Brother Roloff, who had gained national fame for his eight-year fight against state control of his ministries in Corpus Christi, Texas, spoke very informally.

Here is what he said:

> In 1973 the state "welfare" department of Texas, which was neither "well" nor "fair," knocked on my door and said, "We've brought you your rules and regulations." I held up my Bible and said I would have none of their rules and regulations.
>
> I waved this Book eight years. I said just two words that are scriptural — "Get out." I said, according to the Constitution of the United States, you're wrong.

You've deprived me of my rights. Get out.

Now, that's exactly what Azariah told Uzziah. Uzziah came in, maybe with a noble purpose and a fine attitude. He thought maybe in the absence of the pastor, he'd burn some incense, feeling surely that he'd be commended by the pastor when he arrived.

When the pastor got there, he picked up 80 preachers and all of them said, "Get out." Uzziah was a great king. He had reigned 52 years, and they called him the "good king Uzziah." He had done many irrigation systems. His great military had never been defeated. He was a tremendous man. But he made the same mistake Nebraska has made. He was treading on territory that his feet ought never to have touched. His attitude was, "How can you disrespect the highest officer in the land of Canaan? I'm king." Eighty-one preachers said, "Not up there, you're not."

Now, that's where we are. I respect a sheriff who endangers his life to protect our people out in nightclubs and taverns. I've got a lot of respect for the usual law enforcement officer. I never turn one of their children away. But this Cass County sheriff made a big mistake when he came here with his men. Really, he and his deputies violated everything that's precious.

If our pilgrim forefathers were to have been in that building today, standing the way they stood, they'd make us look like wet noodles.

Today will go down as a tremendous day in the freedom fabric of America. I think dead people will be resurrected. I mean dead-head preachers. You cannot imagine how I felt when I heard today that they had gone in to bring you men bodily out of the church and then locked the doors. Here we are, meeting out in front of a church that belongs to God. It's chained and locked, and its pastor in jail.

I just want to say, fellows, victory will come.

When our fight started, 191 Baptist preachers voted unanimously to put everything under the stake. License and all that goes with it. Rules, guidelines and all the rest. The next day the newspaper said on the front page, "The vote stands 191 to 1."

That left me eight long years, and three assignments to the county jail. In 1976 I was on the third bunk of the old jail on the sixth floor, a 1913 model antique jail, and I heard people singing outside to celebrate our 200th birthday of freedom. "My country 'tis of thee, Sweet land of liberty. . . ." And, I thought, what am I doing in here?

Folks, I'd like to give you the secret of victory. Man cannot live by bread alone, but by every word that proceeds out of the mouth of God.

With this, I close. I need your prayers. Physically, I need your prayers. I really do. This has been the most difficult year in my entire life. Fifty years I've been in the ministry. I've travelled more than I've ever travelled in my life, just to keep my head above the water. There are 700 boys and girls depending on us to keep the doors open. I want you to voluntarily pray that God will strengthen and give us real energy to serve Him.

Our Father, bless and give wisdom now. Lead us and give wisdom. Bless the CLA lawyers, the attorneys, and Father, grant that nobody will play the part of a fool. I believe we're nearing the banks of sweet delivery. I really do. I think Romans 8:28 is coming on through. I believe Philippians 1:6 is coming on through. Now, Lord, help us to know that our only hope is to stay with this Book and to live the Spirit of Christ. Thank You for what happens and for these precious men who are here today, and all the people. In Jesus' Name.

Exactly fourteen days after Roloff's visit with us in front of the padlocked church of an imprisoned pastor, he took off in his ministry's airplane. He headed out for another speaking engagement. But God had better plans for him, and he landed in heaven. His airplane plummeted down from 17,000 feet. The press reported that he had encountered a storm.

Ironically, on the very day that Roloff's plane crashed, election day, November 2, 1982, a man named White was elected Governor of Texas. White, we are told, had vowed that he would vanquish Roloff.

"White will be elected only over my dead body," Roloff had stated. That happened, literally.

On the same day Governor Charles Thone of Nebraska, who had at times raised his voice on behalf of Pastor Sileven, was defeated for re-election by Bob Kerry, a Nebraska businessman who has vowed to veto any pro-Sileven legislation that might ever come to his desk. And the Nebraska Legislature moved from bad to worse, from the standpoint of Sileven's interests.

Lester Roloff was ready and God took him to glory. The swift seasons of earth will pass, and soon all of us will be together in that land where there are no tyrants and no tears.

> And God shall wipe away all tears from their eyes; and there shall be no more death, neither sorrow, nor crying, neither shall there be any more pain: for the former things are passed away. And he that sat upon the throne said, Behold, I make all things new (Revelation 21:4-5).

Yes, dear Brother Roloff, *victory will come.*

7
The Pen and Ink Debate

*"The coercive powers of the police state
cannot alter Christian conviction."*

Often it is through the give and take of debate that the
complexities of an issue are best expounded and
understood.

In this chapter I will share an exchange with a United
States senator, a major newspaper editor, and a Nebraska
public school teacher. Then I will share a "letter to the
editor" and a major newspaper editorial which bring clearly into focus the essence of the religious liberty issue which
is being fought in Nebraska and elsewhere.

Late in September, 1982, Pastor Larry Fischer of
Shrewsbury, Pennsylvania, sent me a copy of a letter he
had received from United States Senator Arlen Specter.
Immediately I sensed that the senator was not in possession of some very basic and vital information, so I wrote to
him on October 7.

This exchange of correspondence follows:

September 22, 1982

Pastor Larry Fischer
525 South Main Street
Shrewsbury, PA 17361

Dear Mr. Fischer:

Thank you for your letter regarding the jailing of Reverend Sileven.

Education has traditionally been regarded as a state function, therefore, all schools are subject to state regulation and law. All persons are subject to the law, even presidents, congressmen and ministers. Reverend Sileven can only operate his school if it complies with the same law with which all schools comply.

Thank you for apprising me of your views. Please do not hesitate to contact me on other issues of mutual concern.

Sincerely,
Arlen Specter
U.S. Senator

October 7, 1982

Hon. Arlen Specter
U.S. Senator
Committee on the Judiciary
Washington, DC

Dear Senator Specter:

Your letter of September 22, which you addressed to Pastor Larry Fischer, has come to my attention. I am disappointed that you have upheld Nebraska in the case of Dr. Everett Sileven, Pastor of Faith Baptist Church of Louisville, and I am writing to call certain facts to your attention.

1. From earliest colonial times in America, education
    was a function of the parents and religious institu-
    tions.

2. The U.S. Constitution did not provide for federal
    jurisdiction over education, so early in the last
    century various states began moving in and impos-
    ing controls over education.

3. However, strong and broad-based religious convic-
    tion has persisted to the effect that God Himself
    has mandated, through biblical revelation, that
    parents have a primary stewardship responsibility
    for the rearing and educating of their children.
    Nowhere does God, in the Judeo-Christian sacred
    writings, assign child-rearing and/or education to
    the state. In moving in and taking over education,
    therefore, large numbers of religious people feel
    that the state has usurped sacred rights and pre-
    rogatives which belong to parents and religious in-
    stitutions by virtue of divine mandate.

4. Many Christians today are drawing the line, con-
    victionally, on this issue. They repudiate the
    Hitler philosophy, stated by that madman in the
    words "your child belongs to us." Many of God's
    servants today will place their lives, their fortunes,
    and their sacred honor on the line for the princi-
    ple that Christ need not ask Caesar for permission
    to conduct biblically mandated religious functions
    such as child-rearing and education. Whether the
    school involved is a church-operated Sunday
    School or a church-operated Monday school, the
    refusal to accept state or government approval,
    certification or control will be maintained
    regardless of any degree of tyranny which may be
    imposed.

5. You state: "All persons are subject to the law." But, as our Declaration of Independence states, unjust and oppressive laws must be resisted if liberty is to prevail. The First Amendment forbids government to establish religion or prohibit its free exercise. When government jails a godly pastor for the fulfillment of his religious and spiritual ministry, it is imposing an unjustified limitation on the free exercise of religion. If the supreme law of our land were respected, Pastor Sileven would not be in jail.

6. Adolph Hitler closed all religious schools in Germany in 1936. His government sent armed men to arrest and jail pastors who were saying things he didn't happen to like. Those who will not learn from history are doomed to re-live its horrors.

7. Pastor Sileven and Faith Baptist Church are using the famous Accelerated Christian Education (A.C.E.) materials in their church-operated school. They have submitted their students to nationally standardized testing procedures and have demonstrated that the students are scoring ahead of the national average by a sizeable margin. This information has been made available to the state of Nebraska, but Nebraska still wants to control the church's school. Quality of education is definitely not the issue.

8. Arizona, Louisiana, Texas, Alabama, Kentucky, Indiana and Vermont are among those states which have provided exemptive legislation for those who have deeply held religious conviction and conscience about the matter of operating schools as church ministries without state interference.

9. It is an abundantly demonstrated axiom of history that the power to approve is the power to control, and the power to control is the power to destroy. I call on you to reflect on this principle.

10. County judges in Nebraska appear to possess awesome power. If they want to be tyrants, they can be. "Power corrupts, and absolute power corrupts absolutely!"

11. Timothy J. Binder has written in the *Nebraska Law Review* (Vol. 61, No. 1) a careful 23-page legal analysis titled *Douglas vs. Faith Baptist Church under Constitutional Scrutiny*. He refers to Nebraska's handling of this case as "a severe blow to religious freedom in Nebraska," and exposes the Nebraska tyranny as operating "contrary to the free exercise test which has evolved through United States Supreme Court decisions." Binder further sounds the following enlightened warning: "The decision will unnecessarily place individuals in a position where they must make a choice between their God and their government; it will not be unreasonable for those individuals to choose to obey their God and suffer punishment at the hands of government."

12. A thousand governments, a thousand courts and a thousand armies cannot change Christian conscience. The coercive powers of the police state cannot alter Christian conviction. The Christian is duty-bound to "obey God rather than men" (Acts 5:29) whenever the laws of men are in conflict with the clearly expressed will of God. It is futile for governments to seek by means of police power to accomplish what the cross of execution, the lions of the Coliseum, the sword, the axe, the

guillotine, the burning stake, the torture chamber and the damp, dark dungeon were powerless to accomplish in the past.

In light of these twelve points, which no doubt provide information and perspective which you did not previously have available to you, please reconsider your position as expressed to Pastor Larry Fischer in your letter of September 22, 1982.

Thank you.

Sincerely,
H. Edward Rowe

The following lead editorial, titled "Tactics at Faith Christian Undermine Rule of Law," appeared in the *Omaha World-Herald* on October 22, 1982.

My reply was printed in the same newspaper on October 28. This exchange contributed a certain depth of understanding to the debate; therefore, I include it here.

Mob rule has triumphed at Louisville.

There is no other way to describe events in and around Faith Baptist Church this week, where hundreds of Moral Majority members and other fundamentalist Christians gathered in support of the Faith Christian School. The struggle involves attempts to operate the school without observing state teacher-certification requirements.

By sheer numbers and the implicit threat of violence, supporters of the school appear to have intimidated authorities and persuaded a judge to suspend a properly imposed court order.

"The principal thing is to avoid violence of any kind," said Cass County District Judge Raymond Case in dropping his order that the building be padlocked. "When you've got that many people in here from all over the country whose sole purpose is to resist the law, you have a pretty good setting for violence."

His comments are revealing. Chilling.

So are the words of Moral Majority Vice President Ron Godwin of Lynchburg, Virginia, who threatened "major demonstrations" unless the legislature changes the law during the upcoming special session.

It is a dark day when the threat of demonstrations and the fear of violence are substituted for reason and persuasion. The developments at Louisville have undermined not only the rule of law but also the hopes of responsible people in the fundamentalist Christian community who are seeking a legislative solution.

There appears little reason to raise the issue during the special legislative session. Careful deliberations would be difficult under threat of "major demonstrations." Even without that threat, the atmosphere has been poisoned against orderly consideration of the issue.

The behavior of the crowd in Louisville cannot have helped Faith Christian's cause in the eyes of most Nebraskans, who, through their legislature, are Faith Christian's best hope for relief.

Such made-for-the-cameras incidents as the staged "padlock-cutting" by Tim Lee, a legless demonstrator wearing a Marine uniform, contribute nothing to resolving the issue. Particularly ironic is the prominence of the American flag in demonstrations contradicting what the flag stands for: a nation ruled by law.

The people of Nebraska — who have been subjected to contempt and excessive rhetoric from many of the demonstrators — should be aware that the confrontation at Louisville took a major turn Wednesday.

No longer is it a simple matter of Everett Sileven's willingness to go to jail instead of either closing his school or complying with a teacher-certification rule he thinks is unconstitutional.

Now it is the threat of a large crowd, capable of being assembled in Louisville (or Lincoln) on a day's notice to try to influence the course of legislation in whatever ways its leaders deem necessary.

The threat must be resisted. When intimidation and the possibility of violence become political weapons, there is no safety for anyone under any law.

Following is my reply to the *World-Herald*, which appeared under the headline "Religious Stand Is Fully Valid" in the October 28, 1982, edition:

Fellow leaders of some 1,200 pastors who traveled to Nebraska in support of Pastor Everett Sileven have asked me to reply to the *World-Herald* editorial of October 22, "Tactics at Faith Christian Undermine Rule of Law."

We issue this statement in a sincere effort to clarify our position for the many good citizens who desire to know our viewpoint.

To state our conclusion first, we believe we have not "undermined," but strongly upheld the "rule of law."

The First Amendment to our U.S. Constitution states very clearly: "Congress shall make no law respecting an establishment of religion, or prohibiting the free exercise thereof; or abridging the freedom of speech, or of the press; or the right of the people peaceably to assemble and petition the government for a redress of grievances."

This is the supreme law of our land concerning the matter of religious liberty. It grew out of long centuries of bitter persecution inflicted on genuinely Christian people by state tyranny in league with apostate religion.

The amendment's position as the very first of the 10 that comprise the Bill of Rights reflects the view of our founders that religious freedom is the queen of all freedoms. If religious freedom crumbles, all other freedoms will soon disappear as the light of day at the setting of the sun.

The inseparability of church and school is a very basic tenet of our biblical faith. We believe we have a mandate from God to educate our children within the framework of a God-centered view of the universe.

The education of our children is as much an integral function of the ministry of the church as is the Sunday morning worship service and the preaching of the Gospel of our risen Savior. The Judeo-Christian sacred writings assign the rearing and education of children to their parents and not to the state.

This principle was recognized and practiced throughout the first 200 years of our experience on this continent. The rise of secular humanism (the man-centered view of the universe) in the 19th and 20th centuries culminated in the view, stated by none other than Adolf Hitler, that children belong primarily to the state rather than to the parents. Accordingly, Hitler proceeded to close down all religious schools in Germany in 1936.

The good citizens of Nebraska and of America must weigh well the warning example of Hitler and Nazi Germany. We feel that we must discern and oppose at the threshold any trend toward usurpation by government of the primary responsibility for the rearing and education of our children. We must not allow the secular state to deny our children the civilization-building values of our biblical heritage which gave us our freedoms in the first place.

Sileven's school children are receiving a superior education to public school children, according to nationally standardized achievement test scores. As long as Faith Christian is willing to demonstrate a superior educational product, Sileven believes the state of Nebraska should not interfere. We agree.

But our method of opposing what we believe to be an unconstitutional denial of our rights by Nebraska's Department of Education is called in question.

In characterizing our stand, the editorial used the words "threat" and "violence" and "intimidation" a dozen times. The specter of "mob rule" was raised.

Our reply: Time and time again we demanded that any of our number who would possibly be inclined to violence leave the group. In the early hours of October 18, when Sheriff Tesch and Captain Syslo invited us to the Louisville Police Station to seek a negotiated solution, we promised non-violence.

"We are men of God," I said, "and we will not get involved in a barnyard fight. If any of our men should start swinging their fists, please instruct your officers to stand back and we will restrain them ourselves."

There is not even the slightest basis for the implication that we would have perpetrated violence.

On the other hand, Tesch later admitted that he had even wanted to tear gas us out of the place! Syslo, a truly good man, would not stand for it.

Violence was not perpetrated by us, but against us, when a hundred of us were seized bodily while praying to our God, carried out of Faith Baptist Church and dumped on the ground. When the state carries my body around against my will, for no greater offense than the performance of righteousness, the state perpetrates a hideous act of violence against me personally, against my God, my country and my flag.

Those who accuse us of "breaking the law" must

understand clearly our position: We stand squarely on the supreme law of our land, the U.S. Constitution. We believe Nebraska was in clear violation of that law when it interfered with the religious faith of Sileven and his people, locked him in jail, threw us out of that church, locked it up and stationed armed guards inside.

Appropriate lawsuits will be filed soon, and in due course we believe the correctness of our position will be established.

Those who know anything about the history of our First Amendment will verify our firm conviction that it was incorporated into our Constitution precisely to avoid developments such as the "Battle of Louisville," and that what did happen could not have happened if that immortal amendment had been respected by Nebraska from the beginning of this matter.

Finally, the editorial states that we "threaten major demonstrations unless the legislature changes the law during the upcoming special session." Here again, we have a constitutional right "peaceably to assemble and petition the government for a redress of grievances."

I'm certain that knowledgeable citizens will not seriously rebuke us for invoking our clear constitutional prerogatives.

It is well-known that the *World-Herald* takes a firm stand, editorially, for the First Amendment principles of freedom of the press and of religion. The pastors who stood with Sileven agree with this position.

Our readers will understand, for example, that any such monstrosity as a governmental agency to require "approval" of every newspaper and "certification" of every editor and reporter would raise the specter of impending totalitarianism. Any move by government to approve and certify would be recognized as a move toward control and should be opposed at the threshold by pastors and newsmen alike.

Our point is obvious: Our stand for religious freedom is fully as valid and properly motivated as a stand for press freedom would be. Both stands are based on the very same sentence of the Constitution.

If either of these two precious freedoms should ever be relegated to the rubbish heap of history, the free society that is known as "America" would be at an end.

Ron Marr of the *Christian Enquirer* distributed a petition on behalf of the plight of Pastor Sileven. Headlined "We Protest Attack on Civil Liberty and Religious Freedom in Pastor Sileven's Arrest," the statement that petitioners were asked to sign was worded as follows:

> We as practicing Christians recognize that one day we may all be called upon to suffer persecution or martyrdom for our faith as have our spiritual forefathers throughout history.
>
> However, as citizens of the Republic of the United States of America with its great constitutional guarantees of civil and religious freedoms, we cannot allow that day to come unprotested.
>
> We view with grave concern the arrest and imprisonment of Pastor Everett Sileven of Louisville, Nebraska, and appeal to the President of the United States, the State Governors (in particular the Governor of Nebraska), all Members of Congress and of State Legislatures, the members of the media and all responsible Americans to demand and effect his immediate release and the correction of all those laws and abuses which have permitted this unconstitutional, illegal action to threaten the personal and religious freedom of every American.

One individual who received the petition form wrote an anonymous letter on it, and returned the form to Marr.

The anonymous message follows:

Dear Sir,

I am a born-again public school teacher in Nebraska. I read the *Christian Enquirer*, but feel I must protest your condoning the actions of Rev. Everett Sileven.

Our state legislators, judges and Supt. of School have tried hard to come to an agreement with Mr. Sileven. He refuses to cooperate.

The Bible says we are to obey the laws of the land. Mr. Sileven is openly defying the law and teaching the children in his school to disobey the law. His religious freedom is not being restricted.

I'm sorry it went so far as to lock the church door or to jail Mr. Sileven, but it was his own stubbornness that caused this.

Please read the enclosed clipping and research this more before you take sides with him.

He is disobedient and guilty and enjoying the publicity he is receiving.

> — A concerned Christian in Nebraska

Upon receiving this message from the anonymous "born-again public school teacher in Nebraska," Marr forwarded it to me. Knowing that I had personally investigated the Nebraska situation in depth, Ron enclosed a note asking me to write a response to the Nebraska teacher. I wrote that response on December 6, 1982, and I include the full text of it here:

Mr. Ron Marr
Christian Enquirer
Niagara Falls, New York 14305

Dear Ron,

   This is my response to the note which you received from "a concerned Christian in Nebraska," and to which you requested that I reply.

   I can only say that I am deeply fearful for the future of America if "born-again public school teachers" in general take the same position that this one apparently does.

   Notice, for example, the cliche sentence "The Bible says we are to obey the laws of the land." The basic law of the land is codified in the U.S. Constitution. The First Amendment to that Constitution clearly precludes any such thing as state persecution of a small church and its school for the practice of religious faith, which includes the education of their children.

   Pastor Sileven's position is that the Constitution is clear — and he intends to stand on it. The anonymous teacher who wrote this note to you would do well to consider that the Constitution of Russia incorporates quite a good statement guaranteeing religious liberty. However, the gap between the Constitution, as written, and reality at the grass roots of life in Russia, is a yawning chasm.

   The only way that Christian Americans can see to it that their constitutional guarantees are honored is to take a firm stand for the Constitution and to claim its guarantees in the face of every tyrannical effort by state and county authorities to sidestep it.

Pastor Sileven and a thousand of us who stood with him in Louisville are not "openly defying the law," as this teacher alleges. The fact of the matter is that we are openly upholding the law — the constitutional law of this nation.

Tyranny will possess every single inch of territory that the people of God are willing to surrender. If we retreat in the face of state tyranny, the end of the process will be another Soviet Union situation.

This anonymous Nebraska teacher says Pastor Sileven's "religious freedom" is not "being restricted." The teacher apparently does not realize that the power of the state to approve a church-operated school and to certify its teachers is exactly the same as the power not to approve it and not to certify its teachers. Therefore, it is an obvious and elementary fact that approval and certification means, in principle, state control of religious schools — and that means state control over religion.

I agree with Pastor Lester Roloff who, before his homegoing, visited with us for one evening in Louisville. He summarized his case against state control of religious education in these words: "When the time comes that I take a license from the state to perform the spiritual work of Christ, including the education of children, I will throw my Bible in the first garbage can that I can find."

Your "concerned Christian in Nebraska" simply fails to understand how tyranny happens. Hitler closed down all Christian schools in Germany in 1936. In 1938, he made it clear that he did not want people who were involved with religious organizations teaching in his public schools. Those who will read the history of the Third Reich will note that in many respects the pattern in Nebraska is parallel to that in Germany in the days of Hitler. In Russia today, and in all Communist countries, there is no such thing as a church-operated religious school. Churches themselves must, by law, be certified, registered and approved by the state.

May God save America from the horrors that "born-again public school teachers" such as this one from Nebraska would bring upon this nation with their view that the people of God must go to Caesar for permission to do the work of Christ.

If the state can set up an agency to approve and certify church-operated religious schools, then why should it not set up an agency to approve every newspaper and certify every editor? The very same sentence in our U.S. Constitution which guarantees non-interference by government in religion guarantees non-interference by government in the press.

Religious and press freedoms are absolutely basic to a free society.

The founders of this nation pledged their lives and their sacred honor to inaugurate an era of religious and press freedom and to uphold these God-given principles. Their spirit is the spirit that must prevail in America today, if our precious freedoms are to survive.

Sincerely in our Savior,
H. Edward Rowe

During the Battle of Louisville a very large volume of correspondence was submitted to editors both inside and outside of Nebraska.

I have poured through piles of clippings, and have selected the one "Letter to the Editor" that packs the greatest challenge value to readers who might remain unconvinced of the righteousness of Dr. Sileven's stand.

The letter that gets the "blue ribbon" appeared in the *Montgomery Advertiser* in Montgomery, Alabama, on October 11, 1982, with a headline which read "Decriminalize Religion." The text of the letter follows:

Editor, The Advertiser:

I read with interest the September 9 article concerning a small church in Nebraska and the plight of its minister, who was jailed and his church padlocked, because he refused to discontinue a teaching ministry for children whose parents had chosen not to accept the education that the state of Nebraska has to offer.

Nebraska, through its instrument the district court, interfered because the teachers were not "accredited," and found the pastor in contempt. These church school teachers were obviously "accredited" by the children's parents, however, or they would not have elected to send their children to a church-run school, at extra expense.

A concerned person might ask, "Whose children are they, anyway?" But the real issue is the rightfulness of the state's incursion into a religious ministry. The same First Amendment which protects the freedom of speech that our newspapers enjoy prohibits the Congress from passing any law which abridges the free exercise of religion. Isn't that how we became a nation?

When this great nation was founded, what "accreditation" did the state have for its teachers? Weren't our original teachers also ministers and our first school buildings, churches?

Since the free exercise of religion is not a crime in Alabama, we could come to the rescue of one of our sister states by offering to take these criminals off the hands of the Nebraska authorities. This would alleviate some of Nebraska's problems because: The citizens would be relieved of the expense of incarcerating these criminals; the departure of this criminal element would make the streets of Nebraska safer; the state of Nebraska would have rid itself of one of its undesirable and potentially dangerous elements (who knows just what one of these criminals might do to exercise his freedom?).

Perhaps we could even turn this to our advantage because the state of Nebraska might be convinced to pay us in Alabama for our providing a haven for this type of criminal. The only alternative for Nebraska, as I see it, would be to decriminalize the free exercise of religion. Nebraska must have a strong NEA.

Henri Klingler
Libertarian Candidate for Governor, Montgomery

Another aspect of the challenge has to do with great editorials printed in newspapers and other publications. The prize editorial which I have selected for inclusion here, as a fitting wrap-up to this book, appeared in *The Indianapolis Star* on Sunday, October 24, 1982.

Cited in the masthead above the editorial were two quotations — one from the Bible and one from Abraham Lincoln:

Where the Spirit of the Lord is, there is Liberty (II Corinthians 3:17).

Let the people know the facts and the country will be saved (Abraham Lincoln).

Now here is the full text of our prize-winning editorial which appeared under the headline "Church and State":

The Pen and Ink Debate

The Rev. Greg Dixon, pastor of the Indianapolis Baptist Temple, was one of 85 persons forcibly removed from the First Baptist Church in Louisville, Nebraska, while protesting a court order to close the church.

County District Judge Raymond Case ordered the church padlocked after it failed to obey his ruling that its school, located in the basement, comply with state education standards.

The church holds that Nebraska education regulations violate the constitutional guarantee of freedom of religion. It also asserts that its school standards are higher than the state's.

Rev. Dixon said that if the church complied with state licensure, 95 percent of its school material and 90 percent of its library works would have to be nonreligious.

Because of his prominence in the Moral Majority, a controversial movement, Rev. Dixon is perceived as a hero by some and a villain by others. But, setting aside any bias for or against him, and regardless of whether one agrees with his resistance, it is hard to deny that he raises a basic question of religious liberty.

Essentially that question is: Is it the government's function to decide who is qualified to teach and what should be taught in a religious school?

For the affirmative it can be argued that the state legislature, freely elected by Nebraskans and thus representative of the popular will, perceives that the total state population has a compelling interest in the education of its children and that by establishing certain school standards the legislature is acting for the "general welfare."

An opposing view is that religious freedom, guaranteed by the United States Constitution and the Nebraska constitution, includes the right to teach one's religious views, in one's own manner, whether the majority agrees or not.

What is the proper limitation of government? It's not a

a new question. Through the years political philosophers have addressed the issue and never has total agreement been reached.

Before leaping to support one side or the other in the Nebraska case, it might be appropriate to put the issue in historic perspective by imagining it to have been raised a few thousand years ago.

For example, suppose Jesus had wanted to start a school to teach religious precepts and the civil authorities told Him, "You can start Your school, providing You use teachers certified by the government." Or suppose Moses, establishing a school to teach Judaism, had been allowed to use only government-sanctioned teachers.

In these hypothetical cases, would you support the government's insistence or not? Whatever your answer, the question itself may help you decide what position you should, by logical extension, take in the Nebraska controversy.

8
Occupy for Christ

"We will confront tyranny at the threshold."

Events in Louisville, Nebraska, have dramatized a threat to religious liberty that has been developing for many years.

The lethargy of pastors and churches in the face of government encroachment on Christ's territory is appalling. If we lose our religious freedom, it will be the fault of preachers.

Freedom to serve Christ is always lost by default; never by overpowering force.

The pastors of Bible-believing churches, supported unconditionally by their congregations, constitute the only effective resource in the nation for halting the determined advance of the legislative, judicial and bureaucratic threat to religious liberty.

If the people of God fail to stand for Christ, who else will?

Our Lord Jesus Christ is the only hope of every person on this planet. To the degree that satanically motivated secular forces are allowed to succeed in obstructing the work of Christ, precious people are denied the eternal benefits of the Gospel.

The nobleman who went into a far country to receive a kingdom (Luke 19:11-27) is a picture of our Savior. The nobleman gave certain resources to his servants and said to them, "Occupy till I come."

The word "occupy" in the original language means simply to *conduct business.* The servants were ordered to *conduct the nobleman's business* during his temporary absence. Further, their master held them accountable to handle his business in an effective manner, and to show some worthy results upon his return.

The message is clear. Jesus has returned to Heaven temporarily, and by means of this parable He gives us this command: *"Occupy till I come."* This means we are responsible to conduct the business of our Lord Jesus Christ faithfully *until He returns.*

We are not to set the date of His return and to suspend our labors in anticipation of His coming. We are to be busy at His work *until* He comes. He is to find us active for Him, as productive servants, when He reappears.

Because we are responsible to serve Christ *continually until He returns,* we must confront at the threshold every form of tyranny that would deny us this privilege.

Ours is a life of conflict in which we must *"stand* against the wiles of the devil." The forces which seek to stop us are characterized as "rulers of the darkness of this world," the sinister agents of "spiritual wickedness in high places" (Ephesians 6:12).

Clothed in the "whole armor of God," we are to "withstand" every onslaught of wickedness "in the evil day" (verse 13).

"Having done all," we are to *"stand!"* When all else fails, we are not to retreat, but to *stand.* When all legislative, judicial and legal options have failed, we must *stand.*

Even in the face of imprisonment, torture or death, we must *stand.* This is our mandate from our God. *This we must do.*

"I believe in religious liberty," said an editor of the *Omaha World-Herald,* "but where do you draw the line? Shouldn't you allow any threat to religious liberty to filter all the way through the court system before you draw the line and defy the authorities?"

We draw the line wherever and whenever a threat to our precious, blood-bought freedom to serve Christ raises its ugly head.

We claim our freedom. God is its author; the Bible is its Handbook; the Constitution is its legal guarantee; we are its defenders.

We will confront tyranny at the threshold. This is what we mean by the term "threshold confrontation."

The leaders of God's people must be marshalled and directed toward the solution of the problem of the relentless advance and intrusion of the legislative, judicial and bureaucratic forces of secular government into the sphere of spiritual ministry which belongs only to our Lord Jesus Christ.

God's method of dealing with tyranny is abundantly demonstrated in the experiences of Moses, Gideon, Esther, Isaiah, Daniel, Nehemiah, David, Peter, Paul, and our Savior Himself. The method is accurately described as "threshold confrontation."

Tyranny will quickly occupy every inch of territory from which we retreat; therefore we must not retreat.

Tyranny will take advantage of every weakness; therefore we must be forever strong.

Tyranny will demolish the citadels of freedom if God's people sleep; therefore we must remain eternally vigilant.

Tyranny will corrupt its victims; therefore we must remain pure.

God has reassured us that the weapons of our warfare, although not carnal, are mighty. When unleashed against the strongholds of Satan, those strongholds must crumble.

Let us occupy for Christ.

About the Author

Dr. H. Edward Rowe is president of the Church League of America in Wheaton, Illinois.

Formerly he served as Executive Director of Coral Ridge Ministries, Dr. D. James Kennedy's television organization in Fort Lauderdale, and earlier as Executive Director of *The Religious Roundtable* with Mr. Eddie McAteer.

Dr. Rowe's past experience includes a decade of service as President of the Christian Freedom Foundation and Editor of its publications, *Christian Economics* and *Applied Christianity*.

He also served as Assistant to the President for Public Affairs with Dr. Bill Bright, President of Campus Crusade for Christ.

A previous book by Dr. Ed Rowe, titled *Save America*, was published by Revell in 1976 and reprinted in 1980.

MORE FAITH-BUILDING BOOKS
BY HUNTINGTON HOUSE

THE HIDDEN DANGERS OF THE RAINBOW: Is the Anti-christ in the World Today? Is "Lord" Maitreya the Antichrist? *by Constance Cumbey, $5.95.*
Several months ago full-page ads appeared in newspapers all around the world. The ads announced that "Lord" Maitreya is the messiah and is already in the world. The ads were placed in the newspapers by members of the New Age Movement. The movement is made up of a network of thousands of occult and other organizations dedicated to taking over the world.

Mrs. Cumbey is a trial lawyer from Detroit, Michigan, and has spent years exposing the New Age Movement and the false christ.

WHY J.R.? A Psychiatrist Discusses the Villain of Dallas, *by Dr. Lew Ryder, 152 pages, $4.95.*
An eminent psychiatrist explains how the anti-Christian religion of secular humanism has taken over television programming and what Christians can do to fight back.

SCOPES II: THE GREAT DEBATE, *by Louisiana State Senator Bill Keith, 193 pages, $4.95.*
Senator Keith's book strikes a mortal blow at evolution which is the cornerstone of the religion of secular humanism. He explains what parents and others can do to assure that creation science receives equal time in the school classrooms, where Christian children's faith is being destroyed.

BACKWARD MASKING UNMASKED: Backward Satanic Messages of Rock and Roll Exposed, *by Jacob Aranza, $4.95.*
Are rock-and-roll stars using the technique of backward masking to implant their own religious and moral values into the minds of young people? Are these messages satanic, drug-related and filled with sexual immorality? Jacob Aranza answers these and other questions.

Yes, send me the following books:

_____ copy (copies) of **The Divine Connection** @ $4.95 = _____

_____ copy (copies) of **The Agony of Deception** @ $6.95 = _____

_____ copy (copies) of **The Hidden Dangers of the Rainbow** @ $5.95 = _____

_____ copy (copies) of **Backward Masking Unmasked** @ $4.95 = _____

_____ copy (copies) of **Why J.R.?** @ $4.95 = _____

_____ copy (copies) of **Scopes II** @ $4.95 = _____

_____ copy (copies) of **The Day They Padlocked the Church** @ $3.50 = _____

_____ copy (copies) of **Need a Miracle?** @ $4.95 = _____

_____ copy (copies) of **Yes, Lord** @ $4.95 = _____

Enclosed is: $_____ including postage *(please enclose $1 per book for postage)* for _____ books.

Name _____

Address _____

City and state _____ Zip _____

Mail to HUNTINGTON HOUSE, INC., P.O. Box 78205, Shreveport, Louisiana 71137
Telephone Orders: (TOLL FREE) 1-800-572-8213, or in Louisiana (318) 222-1350

This book is available at the following prices:

QUANTITY	DISCOUNT	PRICE EACH
1-10	None	$3.50
11-24	10%	3.15
25-49	20%	2.80
50-99	30%	2.45
100 +	40%	2.10

Order from:
HUNTINGTON HOUSE, INC.
1200 N. Market Street, Suite G
Shreveport, Louisiana 71107
(318) 222-1350